FIRE

FROM

ASHES

The Reality of
Perpetual Conversion

Joseph Huneycutt

and

Steve Robinson

Ancient Faith Publishing

Chesterton, Indiana

Fire from Ashes
The Reality of Perpetual Conversion

Published by:
    Ancient Faith Publishing
    (formerly known as Conciliar Press)
    A Division of Ancient Faith Ministries
    P.O. Box 748
    Chesterton, IN 46304

Printed in the United States of America

ISBN 10: 1-936270-97-8
ISBN 13: 978-1-936270-97-2

Contents

Introduction

- Reality is the first step toward salvation.

- It is also the second step, the third, the fourth, and the last.

- There is reality we don't want to face.

- There is reality we can avoid for a season.

- There is reality we are forced to tackle.

- Reality is, ultimately, unavoidable.

Do not despair; these sentences need not be understood to mean we are stuck with hard times, denial, or sinful patterns of life. The reality is that not all reality is bad. Hate is a reality, but so is love. Despondency is a reality, but joy too.

Death is a reality, but so is the Resurrection. God is Reality.

You see, we can live in denial or avoidance of the reality of evil and good, hate and love, anger and peace, sin and forgiveness, death and resurrection. Salvation is facing the reality of all of it, trusting in the Reality that is in all—who is everywhere present and fills all things.

The reality is that we all come to God—first, again, often—in some state of being. The Gospels are stories of human beings encountering God, some casually, some desperately, some unexpectedly. Those who have encountered Reality and walked in the Way, often referred to as saints, have left us a witness.

We Christians are all *converts*. Because we have encountered God, we have turned from an existence we knew was a dead end to an existence we know has hope, life. Conversion can be dramatic or subtle, but it marks a conscious change within us.

The reality is that we continue to live after a conversion experience fades. Life is hard.

There is grace in reality if we can and will face it. Sometimes it isn't pretty and we'd rather not see; sometimes it is glorious, but we are blinded by our own will. That is what this book is about: the reality of falling, rising, standing, progressing, and, alas, repeating. Life in Christ is not an escape from reality. Rather, God became Man that we might turn—return—to enjoy communion with Him, the Reality. The Bible says, "He who endures to the end shall be saved" (Matt. 24:13).

This little book is about the reality of perpetual conversion in Christ.

Chapter 1

From Death to Life, Black to White

I knew Mark was a heroin addict when I hired him. He eventually went the way of most of the addicts that worked for me; he just disappeared one day with my tools and an advance. I didn't hear from him for months. The next time he called he was dying of AIDS. "I need to talk to you," he said, his voice a hoarse whisper.

Mark lay in his bed, too weak to sit up. He was a child in the body of a twenty-one-year-old man that looked eighty. His quest for self-destruction was nearly complete. It hadn't taken him nearly as long as some others I knew.

He talked. He told me about his family, the beatings by his father, the conspiracy of silence, the times he sought protection and comfort from his mother only to be pushed away. He told of his early years, how he started drinking and using drugs in the eighth grade. He told about robbing pharmacies. He would just walk in, jump over the counter, grab bottles, and run. He told about robbing appliance stores. He would throw a garbage can through a display window, grab TVs or stereos, and run before the police could arrive. He told about all the people he ripped off, the friends he used, the checks he forged, the drugs he stole from other addicts, the beatings he gave and took, the shoplifting and the breaking and entering. He never got caught.

He told about how, when he needed a fix and needles were not available, he would buy the needles used to inflate basketballs and file them down to a point on the concrete. He eventually got AIDS sharing his needles.

I listened. He got quiet. There was a long silence while he stared at the ceiling. I was about to break the increasingly uncomfortable pause when he said,

"There's something else." I sat and waited. I waited a long time.

He finally sighed and began. "I was drunk one night. Real drunk. And I was driving home. I don't even remember where I was or when it happened. But I hit him. I hit this dude walking across the street.

"All of a sudden he was just there in front of me and *wham*. And I got scared. Real scared; I drove off. I remember going to a fifty-cent car wash and washing blood and vomit off the front of my car and off the windshield. I got sick myself. I went home and stayed inside and stayed drunk for a week. They never caught me. It was after that I started using heroin." He looked at me.

"I killed a guy. I killed him." He looked back at the ceiling, breathing hard.

I waited again. Mark finally looked back at me. "Can I go to heaven, Steve?"

"You believe Jesus can forgive you, don't you, Mark?"

"I guess I don't have much of a choice at this point, do I?" He halfway grinned.

"I guess not." I half-grinned back.

"So, will I go?"

"I don't see why not."

He closed his eyes and his whole body went

slack, like a stretched rubber band that was released.

"Thanks," he said.

"Don't thank me," I said.

"I wasn't," he said.

On the way home I thought of a thief who hung next to a man beaten beyond recognition and yet recognized something in Him that was a hope beyond his wildest dreams. He had nothing to lose by asking; given the situation, he didn't have many options left, really. He took the chance of his life.

Sure, the thief staked his life on it, but it was not much of a life at that point. He was pretty well used up, beaten up, and dumped on the trash heap of

humanity: human trash hanging on a cross outside the city, worthless to anyone for anything—except God. So he offered up his last and only gift, his last-ditch hope against hope that this other hopeless case next to him was who He claimed to be and His word was good.

He was, and His word was.

There is a story about a monastery in Russia where the monks had become "idlers and drunkards." The reputation of the monastery and the Church among the townspeople was ruined by the monks.

During the Civil War, the Bolsheviks arrived in the town closest to the monastery. They gathered together its inhabitants in the market square, and then they dragged the monks out in a convoy.

The commissar loudly yelled at the people as he pointed to those men in black:

> *"Citizens! Townsfolk! You know these drunkards, gluttons, and idlers better than I do! Now their power has come to an end. But so that you will understand more fully how these vagabonds have fooled the workers and peasants for centuries, we will throw their cross and their Scriptures into the dust before them. Now, before your very eyes, you will see how each of them will stamp upon these*

*tools of deceit and enslavement of the
people! And then we will let them go, and
let the four winds scatter them!"*
*The crowd roared. And as the peo-
ple cheered, up walked the monastery's
Abbot, a stout man with a meaty face and
a nose all red from drinking. And he said
as he turned to his fellow monks: "Well,
my brothers, we have lived like pigs, but
let us at least die like Christians!" And not
a single one of those monks budged. That
very day all their heads were chopped off
by the sabers of the Bolsheviks.*[1]

These two stories are parabolic of the Christian
East's view of death as "the blessed curse." Death
is the human being's confrontation with the reality
of mortality, immortality, sin, and judgment. Death
prevents us from living forever in denial of sin and
its consequences in our relationship to God's holiness in eternity. The "deathbed conversion" is the
instant realization of the futility of our life and the
acceptance of our personal responsibility and guilt
for our sin, but it is also a turning to the love of God
in the sufferings of Christ for our sins.

*The Fathers say that the man who vol-
untarily ascribes blame to himself runs
towards Christ's Passion. The Good Thief
is the best example of this: his condemnation of himself worked the transformation*

of his own cross into Christ's Cross, and
he was saved that very day.[2]

Not many of us will have a deathbed encounter with our past before God like Mark, the Good Thief, or the Russian martyrs. The thief on the cross is the exclamation point of the Gospel stories that assure us no one is beyond God's mercy. The exclamation point is comforting, but the reality is that most of us would like to believe we would convert quickly and could stay converted if our death were as quick as our conversion. As Flannery O'Connor said of one of her characters, "She could never be a saint, but she thought she could be a martyr if they killed her quick."[3]

But the reality is, most of us don't live in the exclamation points of spiritual experiences and conversion; we live in commas and semicolons. 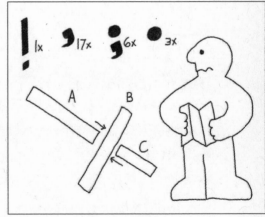 We encounter our self, our pain, our sin, and our God while we have tomorrow, the day after tomorrow, another tomorrow, and yet another before us.

We don't stare into our immediate death but into a future that stretches before us and a path whose end we cannot see nor predict. We may convert but then, instead of being immediately put to death, we find we have to die daily. We take up a cross that doesn't physically kill us but is more of a physical inconvenience because it demands *living*. But the Cross of Christ is a constant reminder that death awaits us all.

One of the spiritual disciplines of the Christian East is the constant remembrance of death as a sobering reminder that we will indeed stand in judgment for our life some day. But the reality is that when we are young, we are mostly oblivious, invincible, omnipotent, and immortal. "Our sojourn on this earth is time given for us to learn how to die, but unfortunately, nothing we are taught in this life enables us to deal with the end."[4]

For some of us, it is not until the ravages of age affect the mind and body that mortality looms and we are taught by our fallen bodily existence, our fragility and sufferings, to sober up about the reality of death.

> In our youth, we rarely think about
> death. Later, we might ponder it rather
> intellectually and abstractly, but as the
> years multiply and the problems of old
> age begin, we behold the warning signs

> *of this great event, because they affect*
> *our daily life in a tangible manner. In His*
> *lovingkindness, the Lord has so designed*
> *our life that we might come to our senses*
> *and be prepared for death when the time*
> *comes.*[5]

For others who are more introspective and experience personal moral and ethical failures in life, the reality of the cumulative effects of sin eventually outweighs the sense of accomplishment, personal integrity, and holiness.

> *There comes a time in a man's life when*
> *he feels that all the works he has under-*
> *taken bear the seed of corruption and are*
> *unable to stand before the gaze of the*
> *eternal Judge. Such a perception leads*
> *to what Fr. Sophrony called "blessed*
> *despair," which, in turn, leads to repen-*
> *tance. This is the "godly sorrow [which]*
> *worketh repentance to salvation" that the*
> *Apostle spoke about (2 Cor. 7:10).*[6]

The Gospels are a string of priceless pearls, each a story of someone in despair who encountered God. Each story is unique, as each pearl and each human being is unique, and yet in them we see the commonality of our struggles—if not in exact reality, certainly in spiritual metaphor. They are stories of conversion, of desperation reached through midlife realizations, of deathbed confessions, of undeniable confrontations with one's own sins, of literal and spiritual darkness and seeing the Light. They are stories of being crippled physically and spiritually and getting up and walking away; of being dead to self, God, and community, hopeless and forsaken, and being made alive again, forgiven, hopeful, and restored. The realization and transformation are never clean and neat nor once and for all. It is a constant struggle, even after conversion.

Take, for example, the witness of a man now known as Moses the Black.

Moses was a former gang leader, murderer, and thief in ancient Africa. However, he became a model of transformation. His is one of the most inspiring stories among the African saints.

Moses lived in the fourth century. He was an escaped slave and the leader of a group of seventy-five robbers. He was a large and powerful man who, with his gang, terrorized the entire region. Moses was transformed after the gang had stolen some sheep and wished to seek asylum in a monastery. The abbot greeted Moses with open arms—such a warm welcome that it had a life-changing impact on Moses the Ethiopian. The peaceful welcome and warm manner of the monks overwhelmed him. He immediately felt remorse for all his past sins, sincerely repented, and begged to remain at the monastery. He soon gave up his old way of life, became a Christian, and was baptized along with his fellow gang members.

Yet, Moses, even *after* becoming a Christian, was tortured by his past and for years was tempted to return to his old ways. The devil fought him intensely with his old habits of excessive eating, drinking, and fornication. Moses also had a rather difficult time adjusting to regular monastic discipline. His flair for adventure remained with him. Attacked by a group of robbers in his desert cell, Moses fought back, overpowered the intruders, and dragged them to the chapel, where the other monks were at prayer. He told the brothers he didn't think it Christian to hurt the robbers and asked what he should do with them. The overwhelmed robbers repented, were converted, and themselves joined the community.

Yet much of Moses' temptation to return to his former way of life became transformed one day when he had a vision while he was confessing his sins to St. Macarius. It is said Moses saw a vision of an angel who appeared with a tablet full of his sins. As Moses confessed each sin, the angel began wiping the tablet clean. The more he confessed, the more the angel wiped, until by the end, after a full confession, the tablet was completely clean. After meeting St. Macarius and St. Isidore, Moses completely left his old ways behind him and became a monk.

Moses was zealous in all he did but became discouraged when he concluded he was not perfect enough. Early one morning, St. Isidore, abbot of the monastery, took Moses to the roof, and together they watched the first rays of dawn come over the horizon. Isidore told Moses, "Only slowly do the rays of the sun drive away the night and usher in a new day, and thus, only slowly does one become a perfect contemplative."

Now, here's a story that might shock you; but listen carefully. The blessing of the Lord came upon Moses. After a while, he became the father and the spiritual guide of five hundred brothers, who elected him to be ordained a priest. When he came before the patriarch to be ordained, the patriarch wanted to test him by asking the elders, "Who brought this black here? Cast him out." He obeyed and left, saying to himself, "It is good what they have done to you, O black-colored one." The patriarch, however, called him back and ordained him a priest, and said to him, "Moses, all of you now has become white."

You see, brothers and sisters, Moses was put to the test—not of his ethnicity or race—but of humility. Race is totally external; it is the interior condition that must be converted, changed. Moses became known for his wisdom, humility, love, and refusal to judge others.

Once, when a brother had been caught in a particular sin, the abbot asked Moses to come to the church and render judgment. He came reluctantly, carrying on his back a large bag of sand that had a hole in it; it dribbled a path behind him all the way to the church. When he arrived, the brothers asked him why he was carrying such a thing. He simply said, "This sand is my sins which are trailing out behind me—which I don't see—and yet you ask me to judge the sins of my brother before me?" At that reply, the brothers forgave the offender and returned to focusing on their own salvation rather than the sins of their brother.

In the year AD 405, when Moses was about seventy-five years old, word came that a group of Berbers planned to attack the monastery. The brothers wanted to defend themselves, but Moses

forbade it. He told them to retreat rather than take up weapons. He and seven others remained behind and greeted the invaders with open arms, just as they themselves had once been welcomed. All eight were slain, martyred by the bandits.

You see, one's conversion can come with a single, simple dying prayer or even a wordless, desperate crawling on our knees to secretly touch the hem of Christ's garment . It can also come through a slow realization of the depth of our alienation from God because of the lifestyle we once embraced and a slow, arduous transformation of who we are. In either case, when you realize you've been forgiven *much*—when you are grateful—you are naturally inclined to *give*—to give even more to both God and man. Forgiveness is *for* giving.[7]

6.20.17

Chapter 2

Suffering the Good, Choosing the Cup

Choices

At some point, or many points, in our life we have a spiritual awakening and we "choose this day whom we will serve." We may inwardly and outwardly declare triumphantly like Joshua, "As for me and my house, we will serve the LORD" (Josh. 24:15).

But that choice, like all choices in life, has consequences. If you choose one woman or one man in marriage, you have chosen to exclude all others from your bed, your mind, your heart. If you choose to have children, you have chosen to exclude sleep, quiet dinners, and romantic vacation cruises from your life for at least a couple of decades. One choice of inclusion leads to a life of denial and exclusion. By choosing Christ, we have chosen to deny self, ego, and sin. In other words, we have chosen one "hell" of a struggle to continually choose Christ and to choose to exclude what is not Christ from our life.

I don't know about you, but give me the choice and I will usually choose:

- the largest cookie in the batch (but without the burnt bottom);
- two slices of bread from the middle of the loaf instead of the first and slightly stale ones;
- to give advice rather than ask for it;
- to spread a story rather than bury it;
- the easy job;
- the seat by the window;
- to click the mouse;
- the glass of Coke from the new bottle rather than the one that sat open all night;
- the slice of pizza with the most pepperoni on it;

- the larger piece of cheesecake (if there are only two left, I might even slice a little off the other one);
- to look instead of turn away;
- to be thanked for giving rather than be given to;
- to turn away instead of look;
- the nicest cherry tomatoes for my salad;
- the second slice of bologna rather than the slightly slimy one on top;
- the white meat;
- an evening with someone I enjoy being with, rather than with someone who needs to enjoy an evening with somebody;
- to be recognized and praised rather than have my good deeds go unnoticed;
- to speak rather than listen;
- the banana with the fewest brown spots.

Given my track record of choices and what they say about me, I think I can safely predict for whom I would have shouted when Barabbas and Jesus were put up for grabs. Which has everything to do with why I need a savior.

Given Jesus' track record, He would have chosen Barabbas, too. Or me. Which has everything to do with why He is the Savior.

What we choose manifests where our heart truly is.

When we realize our heart is bent toward *me* instead of God, our soul awakens.

Choosing the Good

Our fallen nature is manifested in our decisions and choices. Some choices are blatantly sinful and fool no one. Others are more subtle, and they are virtually unnoticeable to the untrained eye or to a clear eye looking in the mirror. Offensiveness to myself or others is not the measure of gross sin. Usually, what other people choose to do that offends me is *my* measure of what is sin.

On the other hand, impressive spiritual feats are not a measure of spirituality. Not even visions of angels are a guarantee of godliness, because Satan disguises himself as an angel of light. Very few people will lay claim to seeing Satan, which is why the Desert Fathers say, "Blessed is the man who sees his own sins rather than seeing the angels."

Sin often masquerades as virtue. Vainglory and

Pharisaism are the fruits of the marriage of virtues and ego. We usually have 20/20 vision for hypocrisy, except when we're looking in a mirror. Sins and hypocrisies that are not my own are the ones I think I would not choose to do, which makes them, to me, scandalous. My personal sense of what is ungodly or godly is not the final measure of what is truly and always ungodly or godly, either in myself or in others. For that to be the case, I'd have to claim that my personal sensibilities are one-hundred-percent aligned with godliness.

Sin goes far deeper than even my own conscience. Someone once said, "A good conscience is not a clear conscience. A good conscience accuses us; a bad conscience will let us off the hook." Sin is the sickness of my fallen human nature, my inclination to self-centeredness manifested in so many small, normal ways that are so easy to rationalize and in most cases just plain ignore. Sometimes it is a low-grade fever that only a skilled physician can diagnose as a systemic illness.

I may not live the life of a thief, shoot heroin with a basketball needle, and murder in a drunken hit-and-run. But in reality, yes, I do. I inject my mind and heart with poison in conversations, through media, and in my thoughts and fantasies. I become

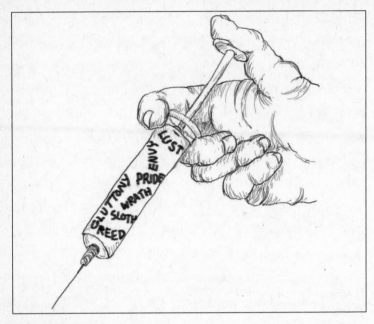

desensitized to human pain, despair, and indignity. The image of God in me and in others becomes darkened in my vision. I steal people's reputations when I gossip. I ransack relationships when I am envious, angry, and unforgiving. I scar myself when I rationalize and cover up my failures. I hit and run when I participate in the murder of someone's character and life by running away, denying knowledge, or remaining silent in the face of evil.

In the Gospels, there were no scandalous sins such as we have today that led to the Crucifixion of Jesus. There were no high-profile celebrity adulterers, porn stars, rapists, or mass murderers. There were only a lot of deeply religious people and a few normal sinners who made normal choices, much the same as we make in our daily interactions.

The Gospel of Matthew tells the story: Judas sells Jesus for a profitable return on his labor. He is two-faced at the Last Supper, faking solidarity with Christ and the disciples. He fakes affection with a killing kiss. The disciples can't stay awake to pray with their friend. They claim they'll stick it out to the bitter end, then chicken out and run when the pressure is on.

The religious leaders are envious of Jesus' popularity. Witnesses at the trial tell white lies. The jury prejudges and delivers a predetermined sentence in spite of evidence to the contrary. Peter caves under scrutiny and denies Christ with a curse to save his skin. Pilate and the chief priests do what is politically expedient to save their status and their system. The mob (of individuals) demands and chooses what mobs incited by ideologies demand and choose.

The soldiers mock Him for fun at another's expense. The executioners just follow orders. The only people at His death are His mother and His best friend. As the Holy Week services of the Eastern Orthodox Church point out, no one whom Jesus had healed, chosen, forgiven, fed, taught, or comforted shows up with a kind word or a tear. All so human. All so ordinary. All so real. All so *me*.

At some point in our life, we realize there is no ordinary sin. We realize that a lot of small sins, much like my own, killed God in the flesh. We realize those same small sins kill our soul. We are being pecked to death by a duck. The weight of a thousand ordinary sins becomes a sack of a million pennies on our back. We realize we are weak, lost, lonely, and powerless. We look for comfort and find that, instead of turning to God, we go back to sin yet again to solve the problem of sin.

Our Little Black Book

Sinning is like dating our exes.

Temptation is my little black book. It is a list of the phone numbers (okay, and email addresses and Facebook profiles) of old friends or lovers I broke up with long ago but for whom I still hold a soft place in my heart. They are people I chose once and then chose to give up and throw out of my life. I  know I ditched them for a reason; they were bad for me in some way. The problem is, I don't know why I still hang onto their number and call them up when I need what they once gave me that I once enjoyed.

St. Peter, quoting the Proverbs, says going back to my old "friends" is like a dog returning to its vomit (2 Pet. 2:22). That is probably one of the most unappetizing images in Scripture. But it is exactly what I do when I go back and eat what I spit out and threw up in my conversion.

The problem with all of us is that if sin really looked and tasted like vomit, the choice would be easy. When Jesus is tempted by Satan in the desert, it seems pretty clear to most of us Satan is offering

Chez Le Chien
• DAILY SPECIALS •
1. Hors d' heuvres
   HURL DU JOUR
2. Entrée
   VOMIT D' DRUNK
3. Le Dessert
   PUKE BRÛLÉE
4. Wine Pairing
   2013 BOURGOGNE BARF

"I wish my sins disgusted me as much as this drawing does." Fr. Joseph

vomit. We know these are temptations because the Bible tells us so. Commentaries make it clear these are metaphorically universal temptations, so we need to pay attention. But in reality, even with a good commentary on our nightstand, it is still pretty difficult to imagine falling for such blatant excesses. Except for Frank.

Frank was diagnosed as functionally mentally ill. He attended church services and Bible classes regularly without incident. One Sunday morning the teacher was discussing the temptations of Christ in the desert. The teacher asked, "How many of you have ever been taken to the top of a mountain and shown all the kingdoms of the world, or been tempted to turn stones into bread?"

Frank raised his hand.

"Yes, Frank?" All eyes were on him.

"That happened to me last week," he said matter-of-factly.

Sunday morning Bible class all of a sudden got *really* interesting. All eyes went forward.

The teacher said, "Well, I have to admit I've never been tempted to turn stones into bread, because I'll fall for the temptation to turn a padded time card, an invoice, a missed item by the cashier, or a fudged tax return into a new TV, a brake job, a credit card payment, or a movie ticket. I've never been tempted to bow to Satan in some spectacular stunt to gain the admiration of the whole world, because I'll bow down for a moment in the limelight, some flattery, to be seen as "in the know" by dropping a little-known fact about someone in a conversation. Heck, I don't need to be offered the whole world, or Manhattan, or even Yuma. I'll fall down for loose change, a moment of amusement, glory, gratification, and satiety.

"So, Frank, it's obvious you didn't fall for the temptation, because you are here with us this morning. Thank God."

Frank smiled. The people smiled. The class went on.

The issue is that our "vomit" is, in reality, attractive only to us. Others' vomit isn't appetizing because ours is made up of stuff we once enjoyed. Temptation is always presented to each of us according to our inclinations, passions, weaknesses, and strengths. They are laid before us as an easy path, a shortcut, an ego-boosting and noteworthy act, a sweet deal, a fulfilling endeavor, a gratifying consumption, a good feeling, and a flattering appearance. Like a dog, we don't discern that the stuff we've rejected stinks, even though others may watch in horror as we chow down on our former passions and ungodliness.

Sometimes we recognize exactly what we are eating and keep eating it as if we were starving to death. And we are disgusted.

Spiritual Desperation

At some point, whether in the act or after the fact, we come to the realization of how far we've fallen, how weak we are, how much light we have closed our eyes against, how chaotic our universe has become, the depth and stench of the filth in which we are immersed. No rationalizations suffice. No resolutions made in the middle of the night are convincing. No guilt is motivating enough. No consequences are fearful enough. The grip of our addiction to our own vomit becomes an inescapable reality.

It is when sin is an inescapable reality that God becomes equally inescapable. It is then that sweet mercy beyond ourselves is our only hope, our only desire, our last resort.

Merciful Spirit of God,
Move across the chaos of this, the deep
and dark waters of my life.

Cast the shadow of Your wings over the
   chaos of my heart:
over the anger at unseen and fearful powers I feel tearing me asunder, powers
   I cannot name, powers I have begged
   You to rebuke, yet they surround
   me still;
over the evil I find myself doing, the evil I
   hear my own voice speaking; the desperate things I do to bring this terror
   to an end in my own vain ways, in my
   own godless time;
over the places within me shattered by
   despair at Your silence at my cries
   and longing for Your aid;
over the places broken because Your
   hand did not stay the brutal, unspeak-
   able, and unseen evils that assail me;
over the sadness that has crushed my
   fragile hope. My faith has been
   ground to dry dust;
I fear for my life. The night is so vast and
   dark, I am helpless against its horrors.
O Lord, hear my frail voice before it goes
   still, before I cannot find the faith to
   beg You any longer for Your hand to
   heal my wound.
I lay this, my chaos, before You.
Spirit of God, pass over the face of these
   my dark waters and let there be light
   once more. Divide the waters, dry my
   tears. Create in me all manner of wild
   and glorious things, constellations of

joy, seasons of exhilaration and rest,
places of angelic praise, places of
deep mystery, places of firm footing.
Let Your Spirit work its blessed and
holy fear within me. Let it gather up
what has been broken and shattered
and create something of Your sacred
imagining. I then will know certainly
You are indeed the Creator, the
bringer of holy order within me, and
the Savior of my soul.

When we have wrestled and lost, eaten the apple and vomited it up and eaten it again, fallen and see no human hand to help us get up again, St. Paul succinctly sums up our experience: "O wretched man that I am! Who will deliver me from this body of death?" (Rom. 7:24).

This is the turning point, the *metanoia*. The moment when we see ourselves so clearly that we can only see God is the moment we do the desperate thing. We will crawl on our hands and knees through the crowd to touch the hem of a dirty robe with an unclean hand. We will start out in hope on the long walk toward home, smelling like a pig. We will annoy a crowd by shouting "Have mercy on me!" and shamelessly throw ourselves in front of God and wash His feet with our tears, no matter who is watching and judging. No humiliation, no distance, no commandment is so great as to kill our hope of being freed from ourselves.

Man calls this *desperation*.

God calls it *faith*.

6.21.17

Chapter 3

The Little Black Book
and the Still Small Voice

A t least he didn't masturbate. Thank God, it
was a good day.

First, a Bit of Backstory

By all appearances, Ted Fisher was a good man: husband, father, Christian. He wore his public garment
well. But, like all strugglers, he had a stained garment. He did his best to hide it, deny it, momentarily

hate it; it wasn't *every* day, but it *was* any day. Any day he was alone, if only for a couple of minutes; any day there was nothing pressing (or perhaps there was much). Every day there was a computer.

He justified it as a stress reliever. He justified it because he and his wife were no longer intimate. He justified it because seemingly everyone was into it (or ignoring it). He told himself he wasn't hurting anyone. (But, by golly, he knew hurt.) His shame, truth be told, was that he justified it. Hell, in reality, Ted was an addict.

Sure, he could blame the kid in Scouts who used to supply girlie magazines on weekend campouts. He could blame the television, the culture, the fashions, the—he could blame lots of things. Mostly he blamed himself. He was ashamed, but never *shamed* enough to break perversion's chain.

Ted used to pray way back when, scared with tears, that the Lord would help him. He swore over and over again that he would never, ever . . . But that was when he was twelve. Now, thirty years later, having put away the old habit for the majority of adulthood, he stood on the edge. At this stage, on this edge, his prayer was that God would not put him to shame. Not to his family or to his friends or to his colleagues or to total strangers.

He had confessed his sin to God. He had confessed his sin so many times that he no longer longed for confession; in fact, he avoided it. He was the problem—not the priest, not the Church, not confession—but there it was. He loved his priest, Fr. John, too much to sully the priestly garment with his filth.

Once, when he tearfully blurted out his familiar sin to an unfamiliar priest, the confessor had told him of the prayer the priest says during the service of Vespers:

> *In the evening and in the morning and at noonday we praise Thee, we bless Thee, we give thanks unto Thee, and we pray unto Thee, O Master of all, Lord Who lovest mankind: Direct our prayer as incense before Thee, and incline not our hearts unto words or thoughts of evil, but deliver us from all who seek after our souls. For unto Thee, O Lord, Lord, are our eyes, and in Thee have we hoped. Put us not to shame, O our God. For unto Thee are due all glory, honor, and worship: to the Father and to the Son and to the Holy Spirit, now and ever, and unto ages of ages.*[8] *(emphasis ours)*

This priest commended the prayer to Ted for his daily rule of prayer. For a while it worked. Ted soon discovered, however, that one can simultaneously justify sin *and* pray words.

He moved around among other priests for confession, hoping not to cause sorrow to his beloved pastor, all the while praying, "Incline not our hearts unto words or thoughts of evil, but deliver us from all who seek after our souls. For unto Thee, O Lord, Lord, are our eyes, and in Thee have we hoped. *Put us not to shame, O our God.*"

Eventually, upon the urging of yet another priest, Ted drove twenty miles outside his hometown to attend a Sex Addicts Anonymous meeting. He thought the distance might provide even more anonymity—even, he was sorry to admit, more *cover* should he find the meeting (or himself) lacking.

It was the first meeting of many that Ted found healing. To this day he can't remember much that was said. What he does remember is what, or *whom*, he found. He found Fr. John. His parish priest sat there among the other men. It was then Ted Fisher realized that, though he might be on the edge, he was not, never was, never need be, alone.

The Fathers teach, "Sin is never an isolated event, and therefore everyone is responsible for their own as well as their neighbor's sins."[9] After all, just because they're not your sins (though all are) doesn't mean they are not someone's. And all habitual sins, addictions, are in essence the same, leading to the same result: either despair and despondency or repentance.

> *When the believer becomes aware of his iniquity, he no longer does anything to conceal it, but he will confess his iniquity to the Lord against himself (cf. Ps. 32:5 LXX). And the Lord forgives the ungodliness of his heart and renews him with the grace of eternal salvation in return for the shame he bears in the act of repentance. The deeper the shame with which he reveals his sins in the sacrament of confession, the greater the power and grace he receives for his regeneration.*
>
> *The presence of shame in the mystery of confession is not only healthy and normal, but also confirms that repentance is offered from the heart—that it is voluntary and deeply humble. Whoever truly repents and confesses his transgressions takes full responsibility for them, without justifying himself as Adam did in Paradise. He does not blame God or his neighbor. Instead, he endures the shame of his sins with humility and courage. This act of devotion heals man by removing the malignant tumour of his pride. He is granted humility, which attracts God's healing grace still more, according to the word of Scripture: "God resisteth the*

proud, and giveth grace to the humble"
(Prov. 3:34; 1 Pet. 5:5).[10]

Once Ted got over his need to be seen as holy in the eyes of his priest and was able to bear his shame before God in confession, Fr. John related a story to him from the early days of his ministry. He had a friend who struggled with cross-dressing, wearing women's clothing. This man's counselor encouraged him to always have some sort of facial hair in order to quell the temptation. This worked for a while, but eventually the man's will became weak and the weight became too heavy to bear; he fell away from the Church, opting to deny reality and live out a fantasy.

Fr. John recalled speaking with his spiritual father, saying, "Why do this man's sins disgust me so?"

His spiritual father answered, "Because they're not your own!" And he was right. Fr. John could justify his own sins, vile as they were, but not those of his brother.

Fr. John recommended the writings of Elder Paisios, of whom it is written:

> He believed that the grace of God was
> the only cause of every good; for every
> evil, he blamed himself out of his deep
> humility. When he saw someone falling

*into sin, refusing to repent, or having no
faith in God, he thought: "It is my fault
that one of my brothers has found himself in this difficult situation. If I were
acting according to Christ's will, then
He would listen to my prayers and my
brother wouldn't be in this unpleasant
state; my wretchedness is causing my
brother's misery."*[11]

Elder Paisios himself writes:

*[A] young man usually observes his
spiritual condition in terms of his carnal
temptations. If a young man has dis-
passion (i.e., no carnal enticements), he
thinks he is doing well, when, in fact, he
may be found in such a state of lethargy
so that he will not be able to discern his
other passions that lie in hiding. God
then allows for the demon of fornication
to humble him involuntarily and, thus,
through humility God approaches him
again. To put it succinctly, the demon of
fornication, with the shock that he gives
the young man, makes him realize that
something has gone wrong.*[12]

Ted was far from being considered a young man—
and yet he knew he was farther still from being a
humble man. The good housewife, husband, faithful son or daughter; the policeman, congressman,

doctor, lawyer, or priest; rich and poor, common and esteemed: *all* are tempted by lust (and the bitter fruit it bears). Sometimes we snap. We fall, big-time. How do we rise? What shall we do? How to make amends? Better still, how to keep from falling so badly the next time? This is the struggle.

There are days when, out of fatigue or illness, we cannot do everything the way we should. It is bad when duties are completely neglected because the enemy gains ground and conquers our heart. In such cases, we must do something, even if it is the least possible, like the good soldiers who when they are not able to

mount an offensive, fire a few shots from their trench, thereby keeping the enemy at bay. Later on, when they find the first opportunity, they attack the enemy with heavy weapons and defeat him.[13]

In a meeting about the besetting sins of lust, pornography, and masturbation, Fr. John asked Ted, "How is your fasting?" Ted was a bit taken aback; he thought it odd to be talking about fasting when what he really believed he needed was an exorcism.

"Fasting," Fr. John explained, "helps temper the flesh and curb our insatiable desire for instant gratification. After all, if we cannot work on the base needs of our gluttonous belly, how can we ever make headway in slaying the ravenous dragon of lust?"

He related the following story:

> And when they had come to the multitude, a man came to Him, kneeling down to Him and saying, "Lord, have mercy on my son, for he is an epileptic and suffers severely; for he often falls into the fire and often into the water. So I brought him to Your disciples, but they could not cure him.'"
>
> Then Jesus answered and said, "O faithless and perverse generation, how long shall I be with you? How long shall

*I bear with you? Bring him here to Me."
And Jesus rebuked the demon, and it
came out of him; and the child was cured
from that very hour.
        Then the disciples came to Jesus pri-
vately and said, "Why could we not cast
it out?"
        So Jesus said to them, "Because of
your unbelief; for assuredly, I say to you, if
you have faith as a mustard seed, you will
say to this mountain, 'Move from here to
there,' and it will move; and nothing will
be impossible for you. However, this kind
does not go out except by prayer and
fasting." (Matt. 17:14–21)*

Who among us cannot improve on his fasting? Ted
thought. His was lacking.

*All those who accept impure thoughts
while pampering the flesh with food and
rest and then claim that the evil one wars
against them out of envy, slander the
devil.*[14]

Ted also came to the realization that, in his all-
consuming desire to surf the internet for naughty
images, he too was choosing to deny reality and
live a fantasy. In turn, this fantasy came to dictate
his reality. No different from the cross-dresser, he
was living a lie. Blinded by his pervasive sin, he was

neglecting those around him: family, friends, and coworkers. As he'd heard in the Twelve Step meetings, it was another version of insanity: "I'll show you, I'll hurt me." First things first—he had to start with God:

> *Therefore, when war with the flesh approaches, if we have done a little fasting and vigil with prayer, and the war does not subside, then we must realize that the problem is elsewhere. We should immediately fall prostrate before Christ and ask for His forgiveness in advance and beg Him, at the same time, to enlighten us so we can realize our fault and who it was that we've hurt or wronged, and to ask his forgiveness. As soon as we humbly ask forgiveness from Christ, immediately the carnal flame departs and we recall the cause, which, in turn, helps us even more to be humble. Then God's grace comes in abundance.*[15]

Often, while in the midst of spiritual warfare, we forget this: the struggle is good. This truth, this remembrance, is contrary to the way the world understands struggle. When we forget that the struggle is good, we make poor choices. Ever seeking the easier way, the lighter load, we come to believe that to struggle is bad, too hard, to be avoided. We may

NEW YEAR RESOLUTIONS

1. THINK ABOUT 2~~010~~ ~~EXERCISE~~ ~~30~~ MINUTES A ~~DAY~~ WEEK
   SECONDS   MONTH

2. LOSE ~~30~~ 20 5 ~~POUNDS~~ OUNCES, BY CHRISTMAS

3. EAT MORE FRUIT, COBBLER AND VEGGIES, ON MY BURGERS

4. WATCH LESS ~~NETFLIX~~ YOUTUBE CAT VIDEOS

5. ~~30~~ 60 MINUTES A ~~DAY~~ ON FACEBOOK
      90   MORNING AND EVENING

6. ~~NO~~ FAST ING FOOD LUNCHES.
   CUT BACK ON

7. GO TO CHURCH AND ~~BIBLE STUDY~~ POT LUCK MORE

8. PRAY FOR ~~10~~ 5 2 MIN. DRIVING TO WORK EVERY MORNING/~~EVENING~~

9. ~~READ~~ ONE SPIRITUAL ~~BOOK~~/A MONTH
   WATCH   YOU-TUBE VIDEO

seek to avoid the struggle with a diversion, such as the internet. Or we may believe we can relieve the struggle with alcohol, drugs, and/or sex. In the end, these only magnify the weight of the struggle. This is the reality of the oft-repeated definition: "Insanity is doing the same thing over and over and expecting different results."

One truth that is easily forgotten is that we never struggle alone. Of course, we have God, the saints, the angels—true. But God also provides family, friends, enemies, coworkers. He provides all for our salvation. Essentially, we struggle as persons in relationship, not as individuals. It is God-pleasing to struggle with all manner of vice within the community of the Church. We need each other, we need accountability. If you don't have a spiritual father, find some mature, wise spiritual friends. It is a good thing to bear our shame in humility before God.

> *Another infallible means by which the believer finds his heart is in accepting shame for his sins in the sacrament of confession. Christ saved us by enduring the Cross of shame for our sakes. Similarly, when the believer comes out of the camp of this world (cf. Heb. 13:11–12), he disregards its good opinion and judgment, taking upon himself the shame of his sins, and thereby acquiring a humble heart. The Lord receives his sense of shame for his sins as a sacrifice of thanksgiving, and imparts to him the grace of His great Sacrifice of the Cross. This grace so purifies and renews his heart*

that he can then stand before God in a
manner that is pleasing to Him.[16]

As Fr. John related, "The devil is not very original; he only uses what works, and if it's worked before, he'll tempt with the same again. This is why we must struggle."

St. Isaac the Syrian writes, "A small but always persistent discipline is a great force; for a soft drop falling persistently hollows out hard rock."[17] But it is when we do not struggle that we begin the slide toward despair and hopelessness.

Sometimes we give up—not totally, but just to that one sin we enjoy to the point of defeat. We may, in a sort of sin inventory, fall to the belief that one sin won't hurt us. After all, we're not a murderer, a blasphemer, a thief, or a gambler. And yet, we gamble. Having convinced ourself that there is no hope of overcoming this particular sin, we take a chance; we surrender that particular struggle to the enemy of our souls.

> *And we kid ourselves that we are, at least,*
> *monogamous. **We're having a relationship***
> ***with only one mistress.** Or, we believe that*
> *one mistress does not constitute adultery.*
> *And, therefore, does not constitute the*
> *only way that we can be separated from*
> *the Bridegroom.*

"Thou shalt have no other gods before me" (Exodus 20:3). This is the first commandment given by God to His people. Therefore one mistress is enough to constitute adultery. Only one paramour is necessary to damn us. And it is that one in which we have lost all hope that God can heal through our unworthy cooperation.

This is the essence of the Christian struggle. The smooth and downward slope and worldly pleasure is what tempted Adam and Eve in Paradise. It is the same temptation of Christ in the desert; it is our struggle.

How is one delivered from such temptations and trials? It is impossible for those who are fallen to walk the path of righteousness without God's grace. This grace is freely given—but, in our sins and disobedience, we are unfit vessels for so great a gift. We must do warfare against the mistresses, the paramours, the Passions. We must, by God's grace, strive toward the Virtues: Humility, Patience, Chastity, Contentedness, Temperance, Liberality and Diligence. How do we do this? As with any God-pleasing act little by little, day by day, moment by moment. This is the essence of the Christian struggle.[18]

Fr. John encouraged Ted to keep a journal, writing about his struggles—in order to analyze and dissect the demon in the struggle and, perhaps, gain some personal insight into his motivations. He cautioned him, however, not to write about the actual fantasies themselves, lest he sin all the more.

> *If something like this occurs in your sleep, do not examine it at all, for it is dangerous. The same applies to any incident in your life (of a carnal nature), which God rescued you from by covering for you and saving you, like a bird from the talons of a vulture. When a young man re-examines the sins of the flesh, he resembles a soldier who, after being saved by God from the enemy's grenade, takes it into his hand to examine it and, while he curiously inspects it, the grenade blows his hands off. Thus, it is a lot safer when we are wrapped up in our dirty sac.*[19]

Speaking from his own experience, he explained that it's possible to take our struggles and temptations and turn them into a craft: poetry, prose, lyrics, and art. In the beginning, this might entail a bit of madness, but as long as we wrestle with the madness, we bear fruit through sacrifice and suffering.

> *In itself suffering is an evil. It is not part of God's original plan for His creation: he made us not for sorrow but for joy—as St. John Climacus puts it, not for mourning but for laughter. Upon some people the*

*effects of suffering are utterly destruc-
tive, leading to nothing but bitterness and
despair. We are not to say that suffering
as such is a blessing from God. And yet,
by the divine mercy what is in itself evil
can be turned to good . . . suffering can
be used. Something can be made of it.*[20]

*Suffering, therefore, has redemptive value
for Christians, not for its own sake, but
because repentance, the awareness of sin
and of the possibility for change, is recognized as the beginning of the spiritual
life. Christians are encouraged to become
aware of sinfulness, both their own and
that of collective humanity, not through
some morbid, neurotic guilt complex, but
because of the revelation of what is true,
beautiful and good, sinfulness being the
distance from it through participation in
what is ugly, false and evil.*[21]

Most times, if we're honest, it's our own rebellious will
that leads us to return to darkness. But ask anyone
with experience: sometimes it seems a demon takes
over, returning us to our vomit. Mind you, this is not
some new sin, nor are we first-time visitors; rather, it
is the old man revisited. Though it may come without
warning, most often the groundwork is laid, the door
left ajar by premeditation. Often, perhaps always,
the still small voice whispers protestations—but the

overwhelming appetite screams to be fed; it is a ravenous spirit leading to gluttony, fornication, anger,
greed—name your poison.

It knows no strangers, only "formers": gamblers,
thieves, drunkards, masturbators, liars, fornicators,
and ogres. These aren't bad people. But it is a malev-
olent menace. Christians are not immune. Although
our vomit, our poison, may vary, the end result is
ever the same: the dark cloud of despondency.

We view our sins, our desires—our demons—as
our secret friends. They perpetually harm us, and we
perpetually seek them. This, in and of itself, is a form
of self-abuse. But we abuse ourselves with all our
passions. They become our masters, we their slaves.
It's a kind of sadomasochism, art imitating life—all

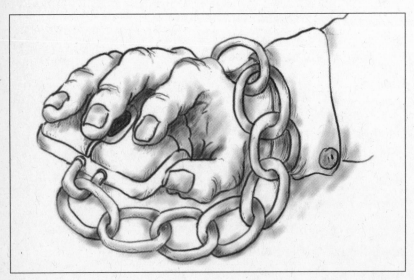

the while complicating, implicating, and shaming by way of our sin. We fall.

Pornography moves one to self-abuse. It is a sin of the senses: "I want that!" I can't have it, but with imagination, I can be a virtual participant. A sweet and permanent agony is "relieved" only by physical abuse. Such an act, this relationship, never consummates or creates. It is fruitless.

With the help of his priest, Ted came to the realization that he was wasting on the internet the time God gave him. Worse than that, he was disgusted with his habitual masturbation.

In a personal letter to a young American, C. S. Lewis wrote:

> *For me the real evil of masturbation would be that it takes an appetite which, in lawful use, leads the individual out of himself to complete (and correct) his own personality in that of another (and finally in children and even grandchildren) and turns it back: sends the man back into the prison of himself, there to keep a harem of imaginary brides. And this harem, once admitted, works against his* ever *getting out and really uniting with a real woman. For the harem is always accessible, always subservient, calls for no sacrifices or adjustments, and can be endowed with erotic and psychological*

attractions which no real woman can rival. Among those shadowy brides he is always adored, always the perfect lover: no demand is made on his unselfishness, no mortification ever imposed on his vanity.

In the end, they become merely the medium through which he increasingly adores himself. Do read Charles Williams' **Descent into Hell** and study the character of Mr. Wentworth. And it is not only the faculty of love which is thus sterilized, forced back on itself, but also the faculty of imagination.

The true exercise of imagination, in my view, is (a) To help us to understand other people[;] (b) To respond to, and, some of us, to produce, art. But it has also a bad use: to provide for us, in shadowy form, a substitute for virtues, successes, distinctions etc. which ought to be sought **outside** in the real world—e.g. picturing all I'd do if I were rich instead of earning and saving. Masturbation involves this abuse of imagination in erotic matters . . . and thereby encourages a similar abuse of it in all spheres. After all, almost the **main** work of life is to **come out** of our selves, out of the little, dark prison we are all born in. Masturbation is to be avoided as **all** things are to be avoided which retard this process. The danger is that of coming to **love** the prison.[22]

Fr. John encouraged Ted to forgo the act of self-abuse even if he fell to viewing pornography. Ted argued that he'd already lost the struggle by viewing the images. "Not necessarily," Fr. John explained. From the book *The Mountain of Silence* we read:

> "According to the teachings of the holy elders, are human beings equally accountable whether, let us say, they fervently wish to steal or when they actually steal?"
>
> "No. You still have a ways to go from the stage of fervent desire to the actual commitment of the act," Father Maximos replied. As he thought of something he chuckled. "Your question reminds me of an anecdote from the life of Saint John Chrysostom. During the time in the fourth century, some very austere Christian zealots, lacking any spiritual experience themselves, insisted that when human beings succumb to a logismos [a desire-laden thought] it is as if they had already committed the act. They misinterpreted, you see, Jesus' words about adultery.
>
> "Saint John tried to no avail to convince them that this was not the case. Yes, sin is committed in one's mind through the logismos, but it occurs at a different stage of commitment. Therefore the accountability is of a less serious nature.

"While he was patriarch of Constantinople," Father Maximos went on, *"he invited these zealots to a lavish banquet. He instructed his cooks at the patriarchate to prepare the most sumptuous dishes. He also sent a message to his guests not to eat during the day because there would be plenty of good food at the table. They did as he instructed and arrived ravenous to the banquet. Then the cooks began bringing the warm and delicious food to the table. Before they began eating he asked them to rise for the customary prayer. Everybody stood up while his deacon recited the Psalms. It went on and on. Twenty minutes passed by and the deacon continued reading from the Psalms. His hungry guests, the food steaming in front of them, wondered whether that endless prayer would ever come to an end so they could sit down and eat. They were salivating with desire.*

"Finally, the prayer was over. Saint John then told his guests, 'You may now leave.' They were shocked and confused.

'Why do you all look so puzzled?' he asked them. 'Didn't you see the food?'

'Yes, we did.'

'Didn't you desire the food?'

'Yes, we did.'

'Hasn't all of your mind and body changed as a result of that desire?'

'Yes.'

'Well,' he said to them, 'then it was as if you ate the food!'

"So with this practical joke," Father Maximos went on, *"Saint John Chrysostom was able to convince those austere but spiritually inexperienced Christians that there is a great distance between committing a sin in one's heart and actually committing it in action."* [23]

From Ted's Journal

Recently, day before yesterday, I had a spirit of carnality overtake me. I did not act on it, but it consumed my mind—a real possession. It began in the evening on Saturday and continued through Monday afternoon. I participated mentally in this temptation/occupation. Then, I could not replicate it if I tried: It was gone. Granted, I asked for deliverance in prayer. Maybe that was the remedy. Thing is, I enjoyed the playful "liveliness" of the demon in the beginning. Then, after becoming like a man in heat, I understood I was possessed and did not enjoy. The still small whimper of my soul won out . . . this time. May God help me in future.

The Self is what was possessed. . . This really seemed an affliction from without—an outside Agent's Occupation. I am not denying culpability. Rather, noting a perception about temptation. Sometimes

it is like playing with fire; other times a
fire consumes us. Not a purging fire, such
as the Holy Spirit. Rather, a burning fire
that blinds us to the reality of carnality.
There is a part of me (mental remembrance) that longs for the possessive
spirit; I remember its "liveliness"—which,
of course, is death. It's a wish, a self-
destructive death wish. Does everyone
have this, to some degree or other?

Temptation comes. Leave it! As they
say in Sex Addicts Anonymous: If left
alone, temptation will leave. "This, too,
shall pass." Instead, often without think-
ing, we act, fall, just like Eve. Just like
Adam, we, too. Getting back up is not
as hard as we imagine. Imagination is a
great and horrible slave master. Yet, we
are slaves to Christ—bought with His
blood. Loved first and we shall be saved
by Him. Love is the greatest. Love: Love
God, love your neighbor (as yourself).
Thus, love yourself. Looking at ourselves
from without, it can look like we are killing ourselves.

There is nothing as temptingly sweet
as an old "friend-sin" revisiting unexpectedly—only to find, again and again, why
the old friendship need end. Old sins are
sexy. New sins (is there such a thing?)
are yet to be labeled. Some we part ways
with early and forever. Others, our paramours, we keep in a closet till either

their siren song overpowers us—or just plain curiosity consumes us. In the end, Crones; that's all they are. There's nothing new under the sun. The promise of the apple is but the tale of the devil and the end of Paradise. It has ever been and shall ever be.

The Tempter says: "You can do as you please—there are no consequences." But that is only because for demons "life" is different. They only "live" when enlivened by our falls. Temptation, for them, is fore-play. They get off on our downfalls.

Cheaters need salvation, too; adulter-ers, too; perverts, too; manic-depressives, too; assholes and jackasses, too. Our problem is we (I) seek to change people, when they need Christ. Christ is always the same—thus it is we who change through Him. Twelve Steps, counseling, etc., are helps toward repentance. They are not the same as repentance. There is no salvation without repentance.

I do have some changing to do. May God allow me to do so in good time. This is where I start justifying staying the same for one more, or more, day(s). Did the Prodigal have days like this? Days where he said, "You know, I know I need to change—but, for now . . . this slop is home." Of course he did! At least I'm admitting I'm prodigal; would that my sins repulsed me! But sin suits *us—ill-fitting—but we justify . . . like pants or shirt that's too small or stained or torn—we wear our own garments (sometimes underwear, hidden from view) and are comfortable. At least that's what we tell ourselves: I'm content wearing, being, the Old Man.*

When you make changes, though the changes are good, there's a sense of mourning and longing for the old, the past—even though the changes are superior. But, as I've experienced, in life, changes prove better with time, prove

beautiful and worthy. Change needs time. Give it time. Time is all we have. All we have is time.

What we do with our time is our life. We cannot wait for a time to come. Time just is. It is always with us, this side of Paradise. Time is what it is—that is, it is what we make of it; just me, God and my neighbor, one day at a time. Little by little . . .

At least I didn't masturbate. Thank God, it was a good day.[24]

Chapter 4

The Way of Christ Is Easy

Greg Johnson's life was miserable after he left the Church, which he did as soon as he was of age at eighteen. He was now twenty-one. If you saw the things he had seen, you'd be miserable about church, too. At least, so he thought.

Greg was reared as a PK, a priest's kid. He witnessed firsthand the darker side of the faithful. He heard the gossip, felt the backbiting, and experienced the politicking, much of it aimed at his father. He felt the darkness enveloping him and, upon leaving home for college, he decided he wanted no more of it. He agreed with a statement attributed to

Gandhi, "I like your Christ, I do not like your Christians. Your Christians are so unlike your Christ," and he left the Church.

The habit in his college apartment complex was to play card games each night from midnight until three in the morning. Tuesday, September 22, was no different, except for church. Not exactly church, but something came up that was hyper-churchy.

His friend, Bill, heard about a monk from the Holy Mountain, Mount Athos, who was coming to the States for a stay at a monastery. Nothing new there; in the Orthodox Church monks visit other monasteries all the time. But this monk had lived forty-three years as a solitary, a hermit, and this was unusual within the Orthodox monastic tradition. Bill suggested they all make a road trip out to the monastery to see if the old monk had any earthshaking words of wisdom, even though he knew the monastery would be packed with others like them "going out to the desert to see a prophet."

Whatever the reason, God only knows why, Greg, in spite of himself, agreed to go.

They spent three whole days at the monastery and couldn't get in to visit with the monk. Greg whiled away his days in the bookstore, avoiding the services when possible. He bought a book, *The Didache* (a short book of spiritual teachings and disciplines of the Church written shortly after the apostolic age), and some pamphlets.

On the final day of their stay, they navigated the dwindling crowds and got to visit the monk. They entered his room at the monastery, received his blessing, and sat down for what they imagined would be an enlightening discourse. The meeting, however, was surprisingly brief.

The hermit, Father Ambrose, made eye contact with each of them in silence. Then, with a kind, loving smile, he simply said, "The Way of Christ is easy. We just make it hard—because we don't want to do it."

Greg didn't hear anything else said in their meeting. Inexplicably, his tears began to stream. It was as if the monk had peered right into his struggle and a relief valve was opened full force. He didn't care who noticed (which was everyone). His friends stared in wonder. Fr. Ambrose just sat in silence and smiled gently.

And then it was over. They each received his blessing and, to paraphrase Scripture, they departed, marveling to themselves at what had happened (Luke 24:12). As they were going out the door, Fr. Ambrose yelled one last thing after them: "Oh! And don't forget to read your Bible! Especially the Gospels—remember to read your Bible!"

Greg knew his eyes had been opened, not to see clearly the offenses he'd witnessed in the past, nor to see some angelic being or spiritual presence. He had seen into his own heart. He recalled an old monastic proverb his father used to use in his sermons: "Blessed is the man who sees not angels, but who sees his own sins."

All the way back to campus, Greg fought the urge to cry full-force. Once he was alone, his tears flowed, and his long walk on the road to healing began. He realized he had distanced himself from the Church, from God, not so much because of "church crap" but because he just didn't want to do what it took to "draw near to God" (James 4:8). It was a resurrection.

Facing reality, seeing our own sins, is the first step toward salvation—the second, third, and final step, too. But so is repentance, our response to reality to which Christ calls us. Greg Johnson came face to face with both those realities in one short sentence from Monk Ambrose. He knew he had left his Father and his Father's house with all of its imperfect elder brothers.

Greg remembered all the Gospel stories he heard year after year in the Liturgy. The prodigal son, the woman taken in adultery, the man born blind, the crippled man by the pool, the woman at the well, the woman with the issue of blood—he'd always known the Gospels told their stories. Now he knew the Gospels told *his* story. He had encountered himself. He had encountered Christ. Now he had to fulfill the command of Christ to repent. What did that mean?

That is the question we *all* must answer when we have seen our souls and have seen Christ.

The Gospel stories are stories of healing, enlightenment, and forgiveness. They are also the stories of the yoke each person was given by Jesus after He had healed and forgiven them. Jesus said, "My yoke *is* easy and My burden is light" (Matt. 11:30). But He also speaks of taking up the cross and following Him (Matt. 16:24). The Cross is an image of suffering and pain and death. It is in the Gospels themselves that we find the understanding of how the yoke of the cross is a light burden on the human being.

Encountering God

Encountering God is finding our true self. The Gospel stories tell of the multitude of ways we experience the consequences of the Fall. Photini, the woman at the well, sought love in all the wrong places. When she encountered a man sitting at the well with no water cup, she thought he was trying to pick her up. It turned out He was God, her true Beloved (John 4:4–26).

The woman with the issue of blood (Luke 8:43), Zacchaeus the tax collector (Luke 19), and the ten lepers (Luke 17:11–19) were religious and social outcasts who saw healing and acceptance coming down the road and made fools of themselves for love. The crippled man lying by the Pool of Siloam had given up on life and bathed daily in the pool of self-pity. He encountered Hope and hoped against hope that life was possible—and walked away (John 9). The woman taken in adultery was near being stoned to death by the command of God, but she was inadvertently cast before God by her earthly judges and found her life (John 8:1–11). Nicodemus, to protect his reputation, sought out a controversial prophet in a dark alleyway and got mugged by God. He was never the same (John 3:1–15).

All the Gospel stories are of God entering the fallen order. The key to the Gospel is that God becomes true human flesh with a true human nature. Apart from this, there is no Christianity and no sensible understanding of the commands of Christ for humanity. St. John says to deny that God came in human flesh is "Antichrist" (1 John 4:2–3). In His humanity as God, Christ encounters the fullness of our alienation, delusion, complacency, rejection, being lost in sin, brokenness, fear, and death. Each person encounters Jesus, the God-Man, the True Human Being, and they are inexplicably drawn to Him.

> How immense is the grace of the divine compassion and condescension that knows no limit? God comes down to the level of sinful men and women; the good Lord speaks with His rebellious servants; the Holy One calls those who are impure to forgiveness. Humanity created out of mud addresses its Fashioner with familiarity, dust converses with its Maker. Let us, therefore, show awe when we sinners stand in the presence of this Majesty.[25]

Those who see Him, God, not merely wrapped in our flesh but truly fashioned from the same dust from which we were created, see something of what they intuitively know is their destiny. They see in Him what, in the depths of their darkest nights, they know they've lost. They hear His voice, and the memory of that ancient sound floods back: it is the voice humans once heard in the cool of the Garden, the voice of their long-lost Beloved, a whisper of their name they've longed to hear again.

They had each lost something of God in themselves, and when they encountered Christ, God in their very own flesh, they saw in a mirror dimly their innermost hopes of what they could be. In other words, in order to know who you are, do not look at who you have been, but at what you were originally created to be. We see original creation fully in Christ. In the Gospels, even nature knew it had met its Maker and in love fulfilled His wishes (Rom. 8:19–21).

This is the divine romance: boy meets girl, boy loses girl, boy and girl are reunited, boy and girl overcome all obstacles and live happily ever after. St. John says to the church of Ephesus in Revelation, "You have left your first love. . . . Remember therefore from where you have fallen; repent and do the first works" (Rev. 2:4–6). What are the deeds of a "first love"? No sacrifice is too great to become one with your beloved. What word can your beloved

however, sincerity is our worst virtue, because in our good intentions we often miss our pride and ego. If we feel off, most of the time it is about the yoke we shopped for, chose on our own, bought, then took up.

Ben attended a men's retreat. As with most men's retreats, part of the weekend involved "sharing your struggles." As each man stood to briefly talk about his sins and burdens, Mike, a new convert, leaned over to Ben and whispered, "Those guys got nuthin', wait until everyone gets a load of *my* sins!" And when it came Mike's time to share, he went on an hour-and-a-half "drunkalogue." By midnight the atmosphere in the room was far from spiritual. Clearly he and the participants at the retreat would have benefited from Christ's command, "Tell no one!"

John was visiting a friend's Orthodox church during Lent. At potluck some people had brought dishes that were non-Lenten and obviously contained eggs and dairy. A young man

LENGTH OF TESTIMONY ABOUT GOD'S WORK IN MY LIFE

HOW MUCH IT'S REALLY ABOUT ME

engaged John in conversation in the line. The young man was a new Christian and was conspicuously picking his dishes, avoiding the non-Lenten fare. John took a little of each so the dishes would not go home untouched and humiliate the cooks.

The young man said quite loudly, "I don't know how you do Lent where you're from, but around here we don't do eggs and dairy."

John smiled and said, "Where I'm from, we do Lent by not looking at other people's plates, only our own."

You see, the well-fitting yoke is the meal that is on our own plate. It is not a one-size-fits-all deal. In the Christian East, the commands of Christ are

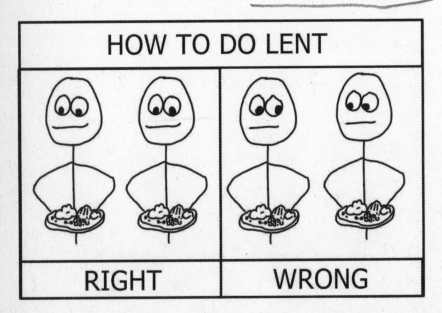

understood to be medicine for the soul. They are prescriptions, and like all prescriptions written by a skilled physician, they are given in dosages according to the specific illness of the individual, with a clear understanding of the dangers of harmful interactions with other prescriptions.

In the Eastern Christian tradition, the prescriptions are usually given by one's spiritual director, a person who is mature and skilled in discerning good from evil (Heb. 5:14). A spiritual director helps one to avoid sin in many subtle guises, such as misdirected zeal, temptations, sloth, and ego. St. Dorotheos of Gaza said:

> *I know of no falling away of a monk which did not come from his reliance on his own sentiments. Nothing is more pitiful, nothing more disastrous than to be one's own spiritual director.*[28]

The self-selected yoke is usually a manifestation of our pride, which is at the root of all sin. There is a spiritual ego condition called *prelest* (sometimes known as *vainglory*) that seizes both the beginner and the mature. The new Christian is deceived through zeal and visions of an exalted spiritual life that is beyond his ability to live. The mature is deceived through belief he has reached the heights

W of spiritual wisdom and praxis and becomes prey to
subtle temptation. And in between, we are just easily confused and led astray for lack of experience.

Metropolitan Anthony warns the zealous about
people who feel "special":

> Even a pious person is not immune to
> spiritual sickness if he does not have
> a wise guide—either a living person or
> a spiritual writer. . . . Surpassing their
> acquaintances in struggles of prayer and
> fasting, they imagine that they are seers
> of divine visions, or at least of dreams
> inspired by grace. In every event of their
> lives, they see special intentional direc-
> tions from God or their guardian angel.
> And then they start imagining that they
> are God's elect, and often try to fore-
> tell the future. The Holy Fathers armed
> themselves against nothing so fiercely as
> against this sickness—prelest.[29]

St. Ignatius Brianchaninov warned young monks
that they should not read many books, especially the
advanced books on the spiritual life, because nov-
ices can never adapt books to their own situations.
He said, "The beginner invariably gets drawn into
. . . pursuing an impossible dream of a perfect spiritual
life vividly and alluringly in his own imagination."[30]

St. John Climacus says:

> *Satan deceives the novice(s) not only
> through the most exalted virtues unsuited
> to their spiritual condition and experi-
> ence. Do not trust your own thoughts,
> opinions, dreams, self-assessments, or
> inclinations even if they put before you an
> exalted holy life.*[31]

Self-diagnosis and self-prescription, even from
the Scriptures, is as dangerous as using the internet to diagnose your own cancer and to pick your
chemotherapy. Sin is a pervasive, systemic disease
and, like all life-threatening diseases, must be cured
skillfully and in the right order to prevent killing the
patient. Applying spiritual disciplines to the wrong
weakness at the wrong time may cause *more* prob-
lems in the long run.

St. Ignatius Brianchaninov speaks about the
danger of engaging in spiritual disciplines without
discernment. He explains simply why people who
may be very religious and do all the right spiritual
things may not be spiritually fruitful, but instead are
ripe for deeper delusions and falls from grace:

> *The ascetical bodily disciplines are to pre-
> pare the soil of our hearts to receive the
> seed of the Word of God and bear fruit.
> No one would sow seed without prepar-
> ing the soil. But if we attend to the dis-
> ciplines without attention to the Gospel*

*and its commands to love our neighbor,
lay down our life, etc., our hearts have
been prepared to bring forth growth but
it will be the weeds of vainglory, pride,
and sensuality. The better the land is prepared through fasting and disciplines the
more healthy the weeds will be. Neglect
of bodily disciplines makes men like ani-
mals, and gives free rein to the passions
like gluttony, sensuality, greed, excess,
lust, and anger; but excess and immod-
erate use of disciplines makes men like
devils (who never eat!) who see merit in
it in God's sight, fall into vainglory, self-
opinion, presumption, pride, contempt for
their neighbors, condemnation of their
brothers, resentment, hate, blasphemy,
schism, heresy, self-deception, and
demonic delusion. So then, let us give all
due value to bodily ascetic practices, as
instruments indispensable for acquiring
virtues, but let us beware of regarding the
instruments as virtues in themselves so as
not to fall into self-deception and pride.*[32]

If we find ourselves mired in sin and despondent,
many times it is due to fashioning our own yoke,
choosing our own cross and falling beneath its
weight, or self-prescribing spiritual disciplines. How
do we keep from falling again? By finding a spiritual guide, a mentor who knows the ways of human
pride, the tricks of Satan, and the pitfalls of spiritual

deception, but more importantly, who knows the way of humility. Humility is where true grace is found (James 4:6).

Finding a Spiritual Guide

Intuitively, we all know we need a mentor in most areas of life, whether in business, relationships, personal growth, or spiritual life. There is no self-aware human being who does *not* seek out advice and direction from other people in certain circumstances. The trick is, how do we know whether we have sought out the right people and whether they are giving us good advice?

There are many personal characteristics of spiritual directors to which we need to pay attention if we are to choose one wisely. Purity of life and humility of heart are two general qualifications. St. Pachomius the Great said, "If you see a man pure and humble, that is a great vision. For what is greater than such a vision, to see the invisible God in a visible man?"[33]

But how do we know if we are really looking at a pure and humble person? There are many ancient sayings from the spiritual fathers of the Christian East that cut to the heart of what it means to be a truly spiritual person, one who is qualified to lead others in spiritual warfare. Here are a few simple "spiritual personality tests" from the ancient fathers and Scripture.

1. How does the potential director handle criticism? St. John Climacus said, "It is not the self-critical who reveals his humility (for does not everyone have somehow to put up with himself?). Rather it is the man who continues to love the person who has criticized him."[34] A simple test, but telling! "Self-criticism" or self-deprecation can come off sounding spiritual, but that is not the true

test of humility. The Fathers warn against "false humility" over and over.

There are people who are so humble they envy the people who know them!

The real litmus test is how persons handle criticism from others, whether just or unjust. Do they speak evil of their accusers? Do they justify themselves? Do they have an air of pride because they are being "persecuted" (a martyr complex)? Do they follow the biblical pattern for dealing with issues among brethren?

2. Does the person *always* have an opinion in conversations or offer unsolicited advice to people? A person who desires to be seen as a spiritual guide and interjects his opinions and observations into conversations is a person to be avoided like

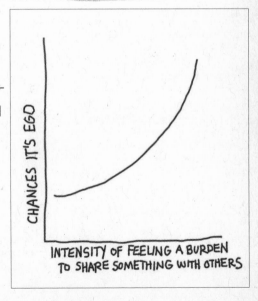

CHANCES IT'S EGO

INTENSITY OF FEELING A BURDEN TO SHARE SOMETHING WITH OTHERS fire. "Unless questioned by the brethren the fathers said nothing that might contribute to [someone else's] salvation; [and] they regarded unsolicited advice as vain chatter. This is quite right; for it is because we think that we know more than others that we speak unbidden."[35]

3. Does the person reveal advice he has given to others or subtly reveal other people's failures and sins in conversation? The classic form of "pious gossip" is "Pray for Sister

Jane, she is really struggling with . . ." This is a sign of lack of discretion, ego (wanting to be seen as "in the know"), and untrustworthiness. You can be sure *your* sins will be revealed in another conversation or prayer circle!

4. Does the person call attention to his personal spiritual disciplines, whether prayer, fasting, almsgiving, church attendance, service to others, or yes, even his humility? Jesus talks about street-corner spirituality (Matt. 6:5). There are subtle ways to boast, and Christians are often experts at the "humble brag"—for example, "While I was at church Sunday morning at seven to set up before anyone else was there, a homeless guy came by and scared me to death." There is an ancient story about a monk

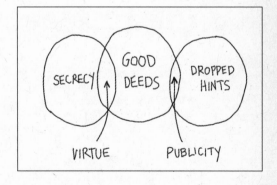

who wore the same robe for years. It had become very ragged and full of holes. He would never accept a newer, clean one from benefactors. An elder visited him and said, "Brother, your pride is showing through the holes of your cassock."

These negative qualities are warning signs of immature or even spiritually deceived Christians who desire notoriety or to be admired. A person who desires to be a mentor but who has not overcome his own pride or who is a fellow struggler without true experience and maturity will do more harm than good.

Amma Syncletica said:

It is dangerous for anyone to teach who has not first been trained in the practical Christian life. For if someone who owns

> *a ruined house receives guests there, he*
> *does them harm because of the dilapida-*
> *tion of the dwelling. It is the same in the*
> *case of someone who has not first built*
> *an interior dwelling. He causes loss to*
> *those who come. By words he may con-*
> *vert them to salvation, but by evil behav-*
> *ior, he injures them.*[36]

Hebrews 5:14 speaks of mature persons who "by reason of use have their senses exercised to discern both good and evil." This is why St. Paul exhorts Timothy not to lay hands on a novice and make him a presbyter quickly lest he fall into the snare of Satan (1 Tim. 3:7). A good spiritual guide must be able to discern the wiles of the enemy, the subtle tricks Satan plays on the ego, both within himself and in those he seeks to counsel.

For the positive qualifications of a spiritual guide, St. Paul in his pastoral epistles gives us a working template for a mature, wise spiritual director. Does the person have the basic qualifications of an elder found in 1 Timothy?

> *A bishop then must be blameless, the*
> *husband of one wife, temperate, sober-*
> *minded, of good behavior, hospitable,*
> *able to teach; not given to wine, not*
> *violent, not greedy for money, but gen-*
> *tle, not quarrelsome, not covetous; one*

why I can't serve in the church

who rules his own house well, having his
children in submission with all reverence
(for if a man does not know how to rule
his own house, how will he take care of
the church of God?); not a novice, lest
being puffed up with pride he fall into the
same condemnation as the devil. Moreover he must have a good testimony
among those who are outside, lest he fall
into reproach and the snare of the devil.
(1 Tim. 3:2–7)

A spiritual director need not be married with children, but he does need to show stability in relationships, relate soberly and appropriately to the
opposite sex, be respected outside the Christian
community, and be the kind of person children like
(yes, that is a Christlike attribute!).

Community: The Goal

When sinners encountered Jesus—the unclean, the
prodigal, the prostitutes, the lepers, the man born
blind, and so on—they all had to reintegrate back
into their communal lives, no matter how ostracized
and sinful they had been. Everything Jesus did and
does for sinners is to make us whole again and
restore the shattered image of God within us. Our

forgiveness, our healing, our yoke, our cross, and our disciplines are all focused on becoming con- formed to the image of God. We are created in the image of God in Trinity: there is no spiritual, personal wholeness and healing outside of our restoration to a communal spiritual life. This is the goal of finding an intimate, mature spiritual guide to help us form healthy, godly relationships within a community of faith to which we are accountable and which will help us stay close to Christ.

← good point. How did mary magdalene feel???

Chapter 5

Fire from Ashes

"I don't remember when I learned to build a fire; I just know how to build a fire. The main thing to remember is that the spark is kindled by the wind."

"What did you say, Dad?" the little boy asked.

Jim Duncan repeated, "I don't remember *when* I learned to build a fire; I just know *how* to build a fire. The main thing to remember is that the spark is kindled by the wind."

The little boy's name was Sam, and he'd been on camping trips with his family for as long as he could remember. Never, not once—though he tried many times—had he been able to start a fire. That was Dad's job.

The amazing thing, at least for a young boy, was that his father used only one match to start the *first* fire—and all the other breakfast and dinner fires, even if they stayed on site for several days, were lighted without using a single match. For Sam, it was magic.

But even magicians require supplies, and one of Sam's responsibilities on every camping trip was to search all around the campsite for twigs, lots and lots of twigs. It always amazed him that such small sticks could help to build such a huge fire. Like the one they had that evening: it roared and roared, warming the Duncan family from the chilly winds of November in western North Carolina.

Sam was determined to learn how his dad performed such magic. That evening, as he snuggled into his sleeping bag, he decided he would rise early the next morning in hopes of sneaking a peek at how his dad built a fire.

The next morning, just as first light illumined the tent, Sam's father stretched, pulled on his jeans, sweatshirt, and boots, and quietly exited the tent. Sam, who'd slept in his clothes, quickly put on his sneakers and unzipped the tent just enough to poke his head out to see.

What was his dad doing? It was the strangest thing: His father was stirring around in the grey ashes of the fire pit. Dust and wisps of smoke dirtied the pristine morning air as Jim Duncan searched for—something. *What is Dad looking for?* wondered Sam.

He could only assume his father had given up the search when he saw him move a bit away from the fire pit and grab a bunch of the twigs and sticks Sam had gathered the day before. He saw his father pull from the bundle a stick in the shape of a "Y." He plunged it into the ashes and dirt in the midst of the pit. He then broke some of the twigs and proceeded to build a little tent-like structure using the "Y" stick to hold the others up. Then his dad crouched down with his back turned to Sam.

Wanting a closer look, Sam quietly unzipped the tent and stepped outside, hoping to go unnoticed. The voice of his father surprised him: "The main thing to remember is that the spark is kindled by the wind."

His dad turned, winked at Sam, inhaled deeply, and blew directly down into the little tent-stick structure. It was dirty work.

Nothing happened.

His dad, a little red in the face, turned, again winked at Sam, inhaled deeply, and blew directly down into the stick structure. His dad sighed and then smiled.

"It also helps to be patient," Jim said.

He blew, *and blew, and blew* . . . until suddenly from, it seemed, out of nowhere—flames jumped up from the ashes, licking the twigs.

Jim acted quickly, gathering more twigs and longer sticks. From a box of wood they'd brought to camp with them, he pulled out bulkier pieces of dried wood and piled them all around the fiery twigs; these were consumed almost instantly. Faster still he worked; no more twigs, he was moving on to medium-sized pieces, greener wood, ever bigger.

And then he stopped.

Sam remembered the time he thought it would be easier to use lighter fluid. But that idea was dispelled when, on another camping trip, the folks at a neighboring site had a roaring fire blazing soon after arriving at the site—thanks to a lot of wood and, Sam observed, a whole container of lighter fluid.

Sam said, "Dad, look at their fire."

"It won't last, son," Jim replied. "It won't last."

He was right. Without a good beginning and proper attention, a fire is never healthy; it never lasts long. St. Isaac of Syria says, "Anything that is easily found is also easily lost, whereas what is found after much labor will be guarded with vigilance."[37]

Grace

Coals (as with the wind, the breath of God) represent the grace of God, which is present in all of God's dealings with us, both as believers and as unbelievers. It is only through God's grace that anyone is saved. This grace is present in bringing us to repentance and in growing us in the image of Christ through humility and continual repentance.

Grace is active in every moment of our life as an unbeliever. It is also active within our lives as believers—forgiving, transforming, and redeeming us. Our salvation begins and ends with God's grace to all before and after conversion. But this grace is not a unilateral relationship. Grace must be freely accepted and willfully acted on.

The apostles often speak of grace (in Greek,

charis) as "power." Thus, grace is a strengthening—given by the Holy Spirit in His mercy and love to aid us in our struggle toward the Kingdom. We participate in grace by submitting our will to God's will, by trusting in Him. We commune with God through prayer and in the grace-filled sacraments of His Church. In sum, grace is the Holy Spirit.[38]

St. Symeon the New Theologian warns us that a Christian

1. who does not bear in his heart the conviction that the grace of God, given for faith, is the mercy of God;

2. if he does not labor with the aim of receiving the grace of God, first of all through Baptism, or

3. if he had it and it departed by reason of sin, to cause it to return again through repentance, confession, and a self-belittling life; and

4. if, in giving alms, fasting, performing vigils, prayers and the rest, he thinks that he is performing glorious virtues and good deeds valuable in themselves—then he labors and exhausts himself in vain.[39]

Receptivity

The reality of the healing work of salvation is that it is not done alone. It is only begun, wrought, and ended in submitting oneself to God. This submission, or *receptivity*, is required in all of our ascetical efforts: prayer, fasting, and almsgiving.

> *It needs to be emphasized . . . that ascetic struggle alone is purposeless; it can only be made meaningful if put in the context of man's overall aim, which . . . is the acquisition of the Holy Spirit. Seraphim of Sarov (Ware, 1993) is quoted as saying: "Prayer, fasting, vigils, and all other Christian practices, however good they may be in themselves, certainly do not constitute the aim of our Christian life: they are the indispensable means of attaining*

It is important to note that we must not mistake the tools for the building. The tools are a necessity, but they are not the goal.

> *that aim. For the true aim of the Christian life is the acquisition of the Holy Spirit of God.*"[40]

> *The assertion is thus, that however gruesome a certain reality is, it is the task of the Christian, through prayer and ascetic practice, to come to the realization of Divine Will in it. Christians claim that just as their true self, the core of their personality, is the image of God in which they have been created, so too their true will can only be reached when it is in harmony with God's will, whatever this may be at each moment.*[41]

Due to the distortion brought about by the Fall, we are so receptive to the slightest temptations, moral lapses, and habitual sins; and yet we must force ourselves toward virtue. St. Theophan the Recluse writes:

> *The Savior said: "Enter ye in at the narrow gate: for wide is the gate, and broad is the way, that leadeth to destruction, and many there be which go in therein . . ."* [Matt. 7:13]. *And He further taught: "If any man will come after Me, let him deny himself, and take up his cross, and follow Me"* [Matt. 16:24]. *"The kingdom of heaven is taken by force (i.e., by forcing oneself and by the earnest labor in searching),*

and the forceful (i.e., those who force themselves to labor without feeling sorry for themselves), take it by force" [Matt. 11:12].[42]

But our spiritual life is often like the old Russian saying: "The church is near, but it's icy out; the bar is far, but I'll walk carefully." As mentioned elsewhere, the struggle is good—persevere!

> Know for certain that submission to God and total surrender to his will and divine plan are a free gift of grace. It thus demands, besides prayer and supplication, a trusting faith to receive this gift. This should be coupled with a longing springing from one's heart that God may not deliver us to discipline for our folly, nor abandon us to our own wisdom. For this reason, we should have an extremely resolute will to renounce our own self at all times and in all works. This should not be done ostentatiously before people but within our conscience. Blessed is the man who can discover his own weakness and ignorance and confess them before God to the last day of his life.[43]

An excellent example of what is meant by *receptivity* can be found in the Morning Prayer of St. Philaret of Moscow (emphasis mine):

*O Lord, grant that I may meet the coming
day in peace.
Help me in all things to rely upon Your
Holy Will.
In every hour of the day, reveal Your will
to me.
Bless my dealings with all who surround
me.
Teach me to treat all that comes to me
throughout the day with peace of
soul, and with the firm conviction that
Your will governs all.
In all my deeds and words, guide my
thoughts and feelings.
In unforeseen events, let me not forget
that all are sent by You.
Teach me to act firmly and wisely, without
embittering and embarrassing others.
Give me the strength to bear the fatigue
of the coming day with all that it shall
bring.
Direct my will. Teach me to pray.* **Pray You
Yourself in me.**
Amen.[44]

The reality is: there are times when, due to our sinfulness, neglect, or weariness, we are not able to do
as we ought in our struggle toward salvation. Mind-
ful of this, Elder Paisios writes:

> *There are days when, out of fatigue or
> illness, we cannot do everything the
> way we should. It is bad when duties are*

completely neglected because the enemy gains ground and conquers our heart. In such cases, we must do something, even if it is the least possible, like the good soldiers who when they are not able to mount an offensive, fire a few shots from their trench, thereby keeping the enemy at bay. Later on, when they find the first opportunity, they attack the enemy with heavy weapons and defeat him.[45]

For example, when he brings us evil or blasphemous thoughts, we should start the Jesus Prayer and say to the devil: "It's good that you pricked at me, for I had forgotten my Christ." When we do this, even if we were to keep the devil near, he won't remain, since he is not so dumb as to work for free and to bring benefit to our soul.[46]

I once confessed to my spiritual father that it felt like I was getting worse in my sinfulness instead of better since my conversion. He said it was possible that I was, by grace, more aware of my sins than in the beginning. Perhaps vigilance had opened my eyes more fully to that which vexed me.

He gave an example of a man climbing up into a dark attic with only a candle. He sees only what is illumined by the small light. Yet if he were to go to a window and draw back the drapes, light would pour in—and he would even see the small specks of dust in the air. In the same way, Christ allows us to see only what we can bear; otherwise, we might despair.

> At the outset of our spiritual life, God, out of love, does not permit us to come to know either our sinfulness or His great benevolence, so as not to despair, especially if His creature is sensitive.[47]

> Hence, the closer to holiness we come, the more clearly visible our sinfulness becomes.[48]

> When man sees himself as he is in the sight of God, his only response is one of repentance.[49]

Fr. Sophrony says: "The more I 'see' God, the more ardent does my repentance become, since I the more clearly recognize my unworthiness in His sight."[50]

A popular story is often told of the believer who once said to God:

"Lord, why have you given me such a heavy cross? Why?" Then he fell asleep, and he had the following strange dream. He was in the most enormous room. All around the walls there were hanging all kinds of crosses: large, small, wooden, iron, marble and so on. And he heard a voice saying to him: "Give up your cross, my child. Choose which ever one you think suits you."

The poor fellow cast off his heavy cross with much joy and started desperately looking for the cross that would suit him. One seemed to him too heavy, another he couldn't lift at all, one was for a child, another for an old man, yet another for a baby. One had thorns, another had needles that pricked. He looked and he looked, trying them all. None of them would do.

In his disappointment, he glanced at a corner and saw one that had been abandoned. He ran to it, tried it, and it suited. Not too heavy, not too light. Just the right size for him. "At last I've found the cross for me," he said. But, to his surprise, he discovered that it was the very cross he had worn before and had seemed such an unbearable burden.[51]

That "Y" stick that holds all the other sticks together is none other than the Cross, ours and His.

Stirring and Twigs

The reality is that we must begin with the fundamentals: prayer and fasting. We do not just begin with these once, but perpetually. Prayer and fasting, stirred by our efforts and the Holy Spirit, are the twigs that ignite the spiritual fire.

Prayer

> *The purpose of prayer is for us to acquire love for God, for in prayer can be discovered all sorts of reasons for loving God. (Isaac of Syria)*[52]

It should be noted that when the disciples approached our Lord and asked how they ought to pray, He did not say, "Just talk to Me." They were talking to Him. (It should also be stated that worrying aloud in Jesus' name is not prayer.) Rather, Christ taught His followers the Lord's Prayer:

Our Father in heaven,
Hallowed be Your name.
Your kingdom come.
Your will be done
On earth as it is in heaven.
Give us this day our daily bread.
And forgive us our debts,
As we forgive our debtors.
And do not lead us into temptation,
But deliver us from the evil one.
(Matt. 6:9–13)

This prayer, said frequently by pious Christians, provides the model for all our prayers: We acknowledge God and His holiness, we pray that His will be done, we ask for that which is essential (our needs instead of our wants), we beg forgiveness and the strength to forgive, and we pray to be saved.

St. Theophan the Recluse lists three degrees of prayer: bodily prayer, prayer with attention, and prayer of feeling.

Bodily prayer is the common work of reading, standing in vigil, and making prostrations. This work requires patience and persistence. It is hard work. Often, the mind wanders, the heart feels nothing; our desire for prayer may wane. However, in spite of these distractions, we must persevere. This is active prayer.

When we *pray with attention*, we are able to

collect ourselves mentally and consciously pray without distraction. When this happens, we are able

to focus on the written words, speaking them as if they were our own.

Prayer with feeling warms the heart, so that what began as thought is transformed to feeling. Words that only spoke to our minds of contrition now become contrition itself. We feel a sensation of the heart with each petition of the prayer. Having reached this stage, we may pass beyond words themselves, feeling that our heart is united with God. Reading and thoughts may cease, leading us to dwell in feeling the prayer itself.[53]

Prayer of St. Philaret of Moscow

*My Lord, I know not what I ought to ask of
    You.
You and You alone know my needs.
You love me more than I am able to love You.
O Father, grant to me, Your servant, all that I
    cannot ask.
For a cross I dare not ask, nor for consolation;
I dare only to stand in Your presence.
My heart is open to You.
You see my needs of which I myself am
    unaware.
Behold and lift me up!
In Your presence I stand,
awed and silenced by Your will and Your
    judgments,
into which my mind cannot penetrate.
To You I offer myself as a sacrifice.
No other desire is mine but to fulfill Your will.
Teach me how to pray. Pray Yourself within
    me.
Amen.*[54]

Fasting[55]

It has been said that fasting without prayer is only dieting, and prayer without fasting is only mumbling. Be that as it may, Orthodox Christians spend a large portion of the year fasting. If all the fasting days and periods are observed and kept, we fast for about half of each year. By fasting, we mean abstaining from any and all animal and dairy products and limiting the quantity we consume.

Our society today is not in any way conducive to supporting such an activity; it suggests to us in many ways and on various levels that we satisfy our appetites and that we indulge ourselves to one end: to enjoy ourselves for the sole purpose of comfort and pleasure. It is indeed a rare exception for anyone to indulge just one appetite. If one is gluttonous in one appetite, then in all likelihood, he will indulge (or overindulge) all his appetites. Furthermore, the Tradition teaches us that appetite and passions are closely related.

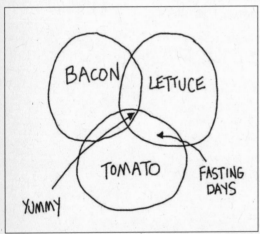

Foremost is the fact that fasting is above all a spiritual exercise, and as such, it needs to be supported by our private prayers, our public worship, and our regular confessions and partaking of the Sanctified Gifts of the most holy Body and Blood of our Lord God and Savior Jesus Christ. This is the reason for the tradition that fasting should be done with the advice and direction of a confessor or spiritual father. *Fasting is a response of the soul to the desire for God, and it is developed over a long period of time.* Fasting is not something we should enter into lightly without any thought or preparation.

The reason fasting should be undertaken with direction is simple. The fasting regulations and rules of the Church are strenuous. We must follow St. Paul, who tells us we must first take milk before we can eat meat; and this is true of any spiritual exercise or discipline. If one attempts to acquire a spiritual exercise without the proper preparation, direction, and support, he runs the definite risk of biting off more than he can chew—literally and figuratively. In such a condition, he becomes discouraged and drops the whole activity. It is, therefore, imperative that fasting be supported by our spiritual life and be directed by our confessor.

But why do we fast? What is the point? Certainly we do not fast for health, beauty, or long life. It has already been stated that fasting is a response of the soul in its desire for God. In addition to the stirring within the soul for God, we fast in imitation of the example of our Savior. St. Matthew tells us that after Christ's Baptism and before His earthly ministry began, He fasted for forty days and forty nights in the wilderness while being tempted by Satan.

We fast, as again St. Matthew relates, because our Savior Himself instructed us to fast and to pray. Prayer and fasting go together hand in hand. One complements the other. We cannot engage in one without engaging in the other if we are to follow the evangelical precepts.

We fast because St. Paul instructs us that we must keep our bodies under subjection. We are to rule our bodies and not let our bodies rule us. We fast for *our* benefit, not to impress God or to manipulate Him into giving us our desires. Fasting *in itself* is not "spiritual"; as the Fathers note, the demons never eat. We grow in grace through fasting as we give ourselves to worship, prayer, study, and meditation until every aspect of life is governed and permeated by the indwelling of God the Holy Spirit. And God the Holy Spirit will dwell in us only if our hearts are a fit dwelling place for Him.

We fast to prepare ourselves for the Kingdom of heaven, as we receive it on this earth, that our souls may be saved, and that we may partake of God's Kingdom fully in the life to come.

> *It is necessary most of all for one who*
> *is fasting to curb anger, to accustom*

himself to meekness and condescension, to have a contrite heart, to repulse impure thoughts and desires, to examine his conscience, to put his mind to the test and to verify what good has been done by us in this or any other week, and which deficiency we have corrected in ourselves in the present week. This is true fasting.[56]

Fasting implies a sense of freedom. Fasting is a way of not wanting, or wanting less, and of recognizing the wants of others. By abstaining from certain foods, we are not punishing ourselves but instead able to preserve proper value for all foods. Moreover, fasting implies alertness. By paying close attention to what we do, to the intake of food and the quantity of our possessions, we better appreciate the reality of suffering and the value of sharing.

Fasting begins as a form of detachment; however, when we learn what to let go of, we recognize what we should hold on to.[57]

Dead Wood

That which we must let go is our sins; they are dead wood. Dead wood is to fire-building as sin is to confession and repentance. It is burned up, purged. In

our weakness, our stubborn will is often strength-
ened, becoming resistant to the healing balm of forgiveness. Yet this same weakness is redeemed into
God-pleasing strength through grace.

> *Because of man's fall from grace, he is*
> *weakened and unable to fulfill the com-*
> *mandments of God. But repentance*
> *strengthens the powers of the soul for*
> *the doing of God's will. [At the outset, he*
> *receives grace enough for him to enter*
> *into the work of his recreation.]*[58]
>
> *Metropolitan Anthony of Sourozh (1970)*
> *. . . comments that the term "weakness*
> *. . . is not the kind of weakness which we*
> *show by sinning and forgetting God, but*
> *the kind of weakness which means being*
> *completely transparent, completely aban-*
> *doned to the hands of God. We usually*
> *try to be strong and we prevent God*
> *from manifesting his Power."*[59]

Most of us dread confession because, like a dog
that returns to its vomit, we often repeat the same
falls and therefore the same sins. A priest of blessed
memory, Fr. John Namee, used to relate how when
people came to him in confession and said, "Father,
I confess my sins only to find that thirty minutes
later I have fallen again!" Fr. John would advise,
"Next time make it thirty-one!"

Elder Paisios states:

> *We have no excuse, however, when*
> *we don't want to repent and confess,*
> *but rather we prefer to remain stuck in*
> *the mud. Some people do not confess*
> *because they have the impression that*
> *they will fall into the same sins. This means*
> *that they simply add more and more lay-*
> *ers on top of the older layers of mud. Yet,*
> *when they stain their clothes, they wash*
> *them and take care not to soil them again,*
> *and when they are stained again, they*
> *clean them once again.*[60]

> *We should be disgusted with ourselves*
> *and work only on our wretched self so we*
> *can first be reconciled with God. After-*
> *wards, great love comes to the humble*
> *servant, and this divine love ignites the*
> *fire of his own love (as much towards God*
> *as towards his neighbor), and he casts*
> *his entire self into the service of others,*
> *believing that he is nothing but fertilizer,*
> *rejoicing that others will produce fruit.*[61]

> *For oftentimes it is egotism, pride and*
> *judging of others with a lack of love which*
> *drives God's Grace away, and the devil*
> *draws near and lights a fire even on our*
> *dry emaciated bones. Thus, we increase*
> *our fasting, spiritual endeavors, our pros-*
> *trations, etc., in order to humble our*
> *flesh, but to no avail, for our flesh is not*

*humbled, and our soul lacks humility
and love.*[62]

*Therefore, when war with the flesh
approaches, if we have done a little
fasting and vigil with prayer, and the
war does not subside, then we must
realize that the problem is elsewhere.
We should immediately fall prostrate
before Christ and ask for His forgiveness
in advance and beg Him, at the same
time, to enlighten us so we can realize
our fault and who it was that we've hurt
or wronged, and to ask his forgiveness.
As soon as we humbly ask forgiveness
from Christ, immediately the carnal flame
departs and we recall the cause, which,
in turn, helps us even more to be humble.
Then God's grace comes in abundance.*[63]

Hearty Wood

Hearty wood represents almsgiving; we can't see
others without a bigger fire. Even those who have
never experienced the brilliant light of a roaring
campfire can visualize its effect on those gathered
'round; it illumines all, partial to none.

In the same light, St. Isaac of Nineveh states,
"Divine care surrounds all human beings all the time,
but it is only seen by those who have purified themselves from sins and who have God in mind at every

moment." Having struggled toward the Light in our ascetical efforts—stirring, twigs, dead wood—we may now add the hearty wood of almsgiving as a healing balm to those whom God has revealed to us. Again, St. Isaac of Nineveh: "The person who benefits the poor finds that God takes care of him."[64]

St. John Chrysostom notes:

> For nothing can so make a man an imitator of Christ as caring for his neighbors. Nay, though you should fast, though you should lie upon the ground, and even strangle yourself, but take no thought for your neighbor; you have wrought nothing great, but still stand far from this Image, while so doing.[65]

> Prayer, together with almsgiving, can furnish us with countless good things from above. They can quench the fire of sin in our souls and can give us great freedom. Cornelius had recourse to these two virtues and sent his prayers up to heaven. Because of these two virtues he heard the angel say: "Thy prayers and thy alms have gone up and been remembered in the sight of God" (Acts 10:4).[66]

> When you are weary of praying and do not receive, consider how often you have heard a poor man calling, and have not listened to him.[67]

*Conversely—Many times, we pray and
God does not listen to us, and the temptation of difficulty remains. But one thing
happens which is even more precious
than being delivered from the temptation:
we receive the strength to rise above it.
That is an even greater miracle!*[68]

In terms of our salvation, the fire we are to build,
with God's help, is not instantaneous. It requires
persistence. This work is never-ending—and yet
the tasks may differ from day to day, moment by
moment. However, the goal, as Matthew the Poor
writes, is ever the same:

*The union of man with God, or deification,
is a legitimate aim to seek. This is due
to the preexisting union between divin-
ity and humanity in the incarnation. It is
Christ, then, who has set it before us as
an aim. Union here includes all the gra-
tuitous means of grace—baptism, Holy
Communion, and perpetual repentance.
Union also includes struggles such as
fasting, chastity, bridling of tongue and
mind. It involves constant prayer as well
as acts of love and humility. It certainly
includes as well God's invisible succor to
those who strive to reach him.*[69]

In a passage mysterious for most believers, St. Paul
speaks of the possibility of returning to our vomit in

spite of the greatness of God's grace manifested in what the Church sees as the sacramental presence of God:

> For it is impossible for those who were once enlightened, and have tasted the heavenly gift, and have become partakers of the Holy Spirit, and have tasted the good word of God and the powers of the age to come, if they fall away, to renew them again to repentance, since they crucify again for themselves the Son of God, and put Him to an open shame. (Heb. 6:4-6)

Thus we must build a strong fire and continually tend the embers of our spiritual life by engaging the spiritual disciplines, even if those embers seem to be cold ashes.

George Mantzarides speaks about the role of the grace of the sacraments and free will in the life of the believer:

> Christ dwells in man through the Mysteries of the Church: Baptism, Chrismation, and the Divine Eucharist. This does not mean that Christ transforms man automatically, in some mechanical way. Man continues to retain his nature.
>
> Christ opens the path of renewal and offers His Grace for man to follow this

Clouds, Bubbles, Fire, Dragons
the heart

*path of his own free will. If man does not
wish to assimilate the Grace of God, if
he does not strive to coordinate his will
with the will of God and to order his life in
accordance with God's commandments,
Grace remains infertile.*[70]

Stirring and twigs represent prayer, receptivity, fasting, and ascetical efforts—little by little. Again, St. Isaac the Syrian writes, "A small but persistent discipline is a great force; for a soft drop falling persistently hollows out hard rock." We must not neglect the little things.

*We must always seek God's help, and
knock at the door and ask, but it is up to
God's discretion when to give grace to
us. When He does not give us grace, it is
not because He is mean, but because He
foresees that we are not able to keep it,
and He does not want to make our lives
even more difficult. He waits until we are
more mature in spirit, so as to bestow
His gifts on us at a time when we may be
able to keep them.*[71]

Rebuilding the Fire

Once, while serving as a priest at church camp, I came back to the campsite unannounced to see the young boys building a huge pile of wood in what they hoped would amount to a great bonfire. The problem was not their intent but the way they had gone about achieving their goal. With supervision, the boys dismantled the large pile of wood and started over, smaller.

In like manner, sometimes our spiritual father will dismantle our spiritual fire, built with good intent through our poor labors, helping us to produce a more God-pleasing, sustainable fire. Like little Sam hoping to learn how to build a fire by watching his father, we too must learn from those who have learned, by trial and error, the way of salvation.

> *Many people think that they cannot find someone to be their spiritual father because they imagine him to be some extraordinary type of man; they want a St. Seraphim of Sarov, and in thinking like this they close their eyes to all the ones whom God in reality sends them. Often times their supposedly complex problems are not so difficult, and they already know that the answer is inside their heart. But the answer does not appeal to them since it demands constant struggle and perseverance on their part. So they go searching for a Godly and automatic wonderworker who can fix all that ails them with one miraculous word; one word and suddenly everything becomes*

*a breeze. These people must be helped
to fully understand the true character of
spiritual fatherhood.*[72]

All of these efforts work together as one, leading us toward the Three in One—Father, Son, and Holy Spirit:

> *Where the flesh is one, one is the spirit
> too. Together they pray, together pros-
> trate themselves, together perform their
> fasts; mutually teaching, mutually exhort-
> ing, mutually sustaining. Equally are they
> both found in the Church of God; equally
> at the banquet of God; equally in straits;
> in persecutions, in refreshments. Nei-
> ther hides from the other; neither shuns
> the other; neither is troublesome to the
> other; the sick is visited, the indigent
> relieved, with freedom. Alms are given
> without danger of torment; sacrifices
> without scruple; daily diligence without
> impediment; there is no stealthy singing,
> no trembling greeting, no mute benedic-
> tion. Between the two echo psalms and
> hymns; and they mutually challenge each
> other which shall better chant to their
> Lord. Such things when Christ sees and
> hears, He joys. To these He sends His own
> peace. Where two are, there withal is He
> Himself. Where He is, there the evil one
> is not.*[73]

In the end, whether we are struggling to build this spiritual fire or to rebuild it, we are not alone; indeed, we cannot do it alone. The reality is that we need God, we need a guide, and we need each other. All along the way, in our limping and stumbling progress toward the heavenly Kingdom, the reality is that God alone is good; He creates, sustains, redeems. It is the mercy of the all-loving Savior that breathes life into all things. Without this breath—this wind of the Omnipotent—there is no purging fire of salvation.

> *I don't remember when I learned to build a fire; I just know that I know how to build a fire. The main thing to remember is that the spark is kindled by the wind.*

Jesus said to Nicodemus, "The wind blows where it wishes, and you hear the sound of it, but cannot tell where it comes from and where it goes. So is everyone who is born of the Spirit" (John 3:8).

Reality is the first step toward salvation. Start here:

> *O heavenly King, O Comforter, the Spirit of truth, who are in all places and fill all things; Treasury of good things and Giver of life: Come and dwell in us and cleanse us from every stain, and save our souls, O gracious Lord. (Prayer to the Holy Spirit)*
>
> *Amen.*

Epilogue

Steve Robinson Writes

''ve lived sixty years as of the writing of this book. I've lived consciously loving God since the age of five. My mother says she knew I loved God before I can consciously remember doing so. In spite of that, I've been a liar, greedy, envious, a fornicator, coward, gossiper, thief, adulterer, drunkard, idolater, and full of pride. I have a track record, and I know I am not yet done sinning and repenting, because I have not taken my last breath.

The stories in this book are about other people, but in reality they are about me, except the parts where those people became venerated universally

nd the flesh

as a saint. I am not there yet, because I am still strug-gling to conform myself to the image of Christ. This is not about a "works salvation" as many interpret the spiritual struggle. This is about the work of faith, the work of repenting, the work of denying self, ego, sin, and temptation. In the words of St. Paul, "I have suffered the loss of all things, and count them as rubbish, that I may gain Christ and be found in Him" (Phil. 3:8–9).

This is the importance of this book for me. When Fr. Joseph and I discussed coauthoring a book about the spiritual life, we both agreed that, in spite of our reputations of being "Ortho-comedians," it had to be real. Being real means looking into the dark places of the fallen human being. The first place to look is within ourselves. Because I know myself, I know I cannot point a finger at another. I can only point out that we share a desperate spiritual strug-gle that is common to us all.

The readers who follow my blog, *Pithless Thoughts*, and my podcast, *Steve the Builder*, know a little bit about my past, my struggles, and my sins. I lay no claim to saying anything new in the parts I wrote in this short book. It has all been said more eloquently and insightfully by many saints in Christ from ages past. But if this has touched a soul and pointed someone to hope and toward the Cross and the Resurrection, then to God be the glory, even if I check once in a while on the sales statistics.

> *The world in which we now live, no matter how beautiful it may be, is like a veil that separates us from both the kingdom of God and the kingdom of darkness. There are times, however, when the shadow of the kingdom of darkness is cast over us; sometimes we receive the luminous rays of the kingdom of light, which console and sustain us. We must simply keep the gift of God in our heart, so as to be able to stand in that day when the Lord will shake heaven and earth. Then all those things which are created will pass away, and only those things that are marked by the uncreated grace of His Cross and Resurrection will remain forever.*[74]

Joseph Huneycutt Writes

Back in November of 2011, during a women's retreat at St. John Church, Memphis, Tennessee, God—who is always good—allowed a Memphis woman to pronounce a fitting key to the work at hand. She said, "Sometimes, I think, the Church is better at dealing with new sinners than with old ones." She went on to explain that a felon right out of prison, who

might still be involved in a shady lifestyle and det-
rimental habits, is often more welcomed, helped,
and nurtured than the long-time member who has
suddenly taken a hard fall, developed or returned to
bad habits, or taken a turn from light to dark.

Deeper still, within the heart, is the need for
seasoned Christians to be helped back toward
God-pleasing health—and, eventually, to the Kingdom. For many (perhaps most—I can only speak
for myself), this is not a onetime do-over. For all
who struggle, it is the same struggle, perpetually:
fall down, get up. However, it is not just a matter
of getting up after falling; we must be facing the
right direction. Sometimes, just remaining *standing*
is progress in and of itself.

Standing is a struggle. Were it not for the specter
of my past failures, I believe I would stand firmer in
the face of more challenges. I use that as an excuse.
Rather, in my mind, it always looms large when I get
idealistic. Other times I have viewed the past as a
Godsend to keep me humble. But God doesn't send
failures; I am responsible for those. There is nothing
that the past can do *to* me—I do the past to myself.
There are other dragons. That one, the past, is dead.
Let it be. But, oh no; I like to resurrect it to try to
undo it. But the undoing only brings fear—because

a resurrected monster is unpredictable, whereas a dead one, though personal pain remains, is still dead.

God not only tolerates us, He gives us blessing and beauty. Because of this alone I should struggle. At the very least, for this alone I should love because He first loved. I know the struggle, yet I am constantly forgetting the fearful Day when I must stand before my Creator and give answer. Instead, *I waste time* in fearing the day at hand, petty politics, ill health, worldly cares, and death. What I should fear is showing up short when the talents are tallied.

For the most part, dear reader, I've learned that I need you, I need God, and I need the Church. If this little book has been of help to you, glory to God! If, in reality, it has done nothing more than engender your pity and prayers, I have selfishly accomplished a great deal and shall be ever in your debt.

Glory to God for all things!

Notes

1   Arch. Tikhon (Shevkunov), *Everyday Saints and Other Stories*, trans. Julian Henry Lowenfield (Dallas, TX: Pokrov Publications, 2012), p. 215.

2   Arch. Zacharias, *The Hidden Man of the Heart (1 Peter 3:4): The Cultivation of the Heart in Orthodox Christian Anthropology* (Dalton, PA: Mount Thabor Publishing, 2008), p. 55.

3   O'Connor, Flannery, *The Complete Stories* (New York: Noonday Press, 1972), p. 243.

4   Zacharias, p. 26.

5   Zacharias, p. 32.

6   Zacharias, p. 91.

7   Today, Moses the Black is considered not only the patron saint of African-Americans but a model for us all. St. Moses is a model of Christian humility, love, and forgiveness.

8   *Liturgikon: The Book of Divine Services for the Priest and Deacon,* 3rd ed. (Englewood, NJ: The Antiochian Orthodox Christian Archdiocese of North America, 2010), p. 23.

9   Gaist, Byron J., *Creative Suffering and the Wounded Healer—Analytical Psychology and Orthodox Christian Theology* (Rollinsford, NH: Orthodox Research Institute, 2010), p. 230.

10 Zacharias, p. 53.

11   Gaist, p. 230.

12   Paisios (Elder) of Mount Athos, *Epistles* (Thessaloniki, Greece: Holy Monastery of the Evangelist John the Theologian, 2002), p. 80.

13   Paisios, op. cit., p. 69.

14   Paisios, p. 102.

15   Paisios, p. 79.

16   Zacharias, p. 8.

17   St. Isaac the Syrian, *The Ascetical Homilies of Saint Isaac the Syrian* (Boston: Holy Transfiguration Monastery, 1984), p. 234.

18   Huneycutt, Joseph David, *Defeating Sin—Overcoming Our Passions and Changing Forever* (Salisbury, MA: Regina Orthodox Press, 2007), pp. 89–93.

19   Paisios, pp. 73–74.

20   Gaist, pp. 218–219.

21   Gaist, p. 219.

22   From a letter to Keith Masson found in *Collected Letters of C. S. Lewis: Vol 3* (Cambridge University Press, 2007), pp. 758–59 (emphasis original).

23   Markides, Kyriacos, *The Mountain of Silence: A Search for Orthodox Spirituality* (New York: Image/Doubleday, 2002), p. 128.

24   Due to its omnipresence in our current societal struggle, the authors chose internet porn addiction as the focus for this chapter. But the wasting of time is common to all internet addictions—gaming, gambling, shopping, news sleuthing, entertainment and gossip sites, etc. The same can be said concerning drug or alcohol addiction. As one spiritual father said, "Stopping drinking is as easy as not picking up the glass." And this is true on multiple levels; there's nothing easy about breaking the chains of addiction, no matter the poison. This chapter was reviewed by males and females who struggle with various forms of addiction or "sexual deviancy." Although journaling or twelve-step help might not be the answer for everyone, the consensus was that it was helpful just to be addressing the issue. The authors have given a few suggestions that have worked for others. No *cure* is offered, as

everyone struggles differently. It is recommended that one speak with a confessor or spiritual father in order to address the struggle and, of course, struggle together with accountability.

25 St. Martyrius [*The Syriac Fathers on Prayer and the Spiritual Life*]. http://tasbeha.org/content/community/index.php?topic=592.65;wap2

26 Bryan Adams, http://www.azlyrics.com/lyrics/bryanadams/everythingidoidoitforyou.html

27 St. Diadichos of Photiki [On Spiritual Knowledge and Discrimination, *Philokalia,* vol. 1]. http://ststylianos.org/prayer/resources/philokalia/diadochos.html

28 Dorotheos of Gaza [*Discourses and Sayings*, Chapter 22: Maxims on the Spiritual Life] http://www.antiochian.org/node/17172

29 Met. Anthony Khrapovitsky, http://debatingchristianity.com/forum/viewtopic.php?t=7186

30 Bp. Ignatius Brianchaninov, *The Arena*. http://www.christianforums.com/t7314662/

31 http://www.euphrosynoscafe.com/forum/viewtopic.php?f=12&p=30359&start=0&st=0&sk=t&sd=a

32 Bp. Ignatius Brianchaninov, *The Arena*. http://www.christianforums.com/t7314662/

33 http://avowofconversation.wordpress.com/2013/05/15/what-is-greater-than-such-a-vision/

34 http://www.pravoslavie.ru/english/45693.htm

35 Ss. Peter of Damaskos, Nikodemos, and Makarios, *The Philokalia,* vol. 3, eds. and trans. G.E.H. Palmer, Philip Sherrard, Kallistos Ware (London: Faber and Faber, 1984), p. 186.

36 http://www.fordham.edu/halsall/source/hesychasm1.asp

37 http://www.22ndcenturymedia.com/Articles-Opinion-c-2012-04-06-239905.114133-The-gift-of-god.html

38 Huneycutt, p. 192.

39 Pomazansky, Michael, *Orthodox Dogmatic Theology*, ed. and trans. Hieromonk Seraphim Rose (Platina, CA: St.

Herman of Alaska Brotherhood, 1997), pp. 260–261.

40 Gaist, p. 214 (italics ours).

41 Gaist, p. 253 (cf. Hopko, 2006; pp. 39–41).

42 http://www.stsymeon.com/theoph1.html

43 Matthew the Poor, *Orthodox Prayer Life—The Interior Way* (Yonkers, NY: St. Vladimir's Seminary Press, 2003), p. 123.

44 http://idrathernotsay123.wordpress.com/2007/09/07/ the-morning-prayer-of-metropolitan-philaret-of-moscow/

45 Paisios, p. 69.

46 Paisios, p. 72.

47 Paisios, p. 103.

48 Gaist, p. 231.

49 Zacharias, p. 67.

50 Zacharias, p. 173.

51 Gaist, pp. 191–192.

52 http://www.orthodox.net/gleanings/love_of_god.html

53 Igumen Chariton, *The Art of Prayer: An Orthodox Anthology* (London: Faber & Faber, 1997), p. 52.

54 Adapted from http://www.orthodox.net/trebnic/of-philar- et-of-moscow.html

55 The following section is adapted from Archimandrite Damian (Hart), October 1984 (excerpted from unpublished article). http://southern-orthodoxy.blogspot.com/2009/11/ on-fasting-by-archimandrite-damian-hart.html

56 Often attributed to St. John Chrysostom; source unknown.

57 Patriarch Bartholomew, *Encountering the Mystery— Understanding Orthodox Christianity Today* (New York: Doubleday, 2008), p. 82.

58 Zacharias, p. 117.

59 Gaist, p. 190.

60 Paisios, p. 91.

61 Paisios, p. 77.

62 Paisios, p. 79.

63 Paisios, p. 79.

64 Taken from "The Wisdom of St. Isaac of Nineveh." http:// southern-orthodoxy.blogspot.com/2007/06/this-just-in- st-isaac-of-syria.html

65 St. John Chrysostom: http://www.newadvent.org/ fathers/220125.htm

66 Weaver, John A., *Cathechetical Themes in the Post- baptismal Teaching of St. John Chrysostom* (Washington, DC: The Catholic University of America, 1964), p. 84.

67 Homily XI on I Thessalonians; quoted from Brown, Peter, *The Body and Society* (New York: Columbia University Press, 1988), p. 310.

68 Zacharias, p. 109.

69 Matthew the Poor, p. 107.

70 Archbp. Chrysostomos, (November 27, 2004, p. 1). Ἐπι τη ιερα μνημη του Ἁγιου Γρηγοριου του Παλαμα (14 Νοεμβριου): Ἡ χριστοειδης μεταμορφωση του νου" (On the occasion of the commemoration of St. Gregory Palamas [Nov. 14]: The transformation of the mind into the likeness of Christ). Synod in Resistance.org. Retrieved May 27, 2013 from http://www.synodinresistance.org/Theology_ el/3e3012GrhgorPal.pdf

71 Zacharias, p. 149.

72 Ware, Kallistos, *The Inner Kingdom: Volume 1 of the Collected Works* (Yonkers, NY: St. Vladimir's Seminary Press, 2000), p. 145.

73 Tertullian (2nd–3rd c.) http://www.ccel.org/ccel/schaff/ anf04.iii.v.ii.viii.html

74 Zacharias, p. 192.

About the Authors

Fr. Joseph Huneycutt was reared a Southern Baptist (which, he adds, is a requirement in North Carolina). He spent a decade as an Episcopalian before converting to Orthodoxy in 1993. Fr. Joseph hosts a blog called *Orthodixie* and delivers a podcast on Ancient Faith Radio by the same name. In addition to speaking engagements, retreats, and conferences, Fr. Joseph is best known for his books: *One Flew Over the Onion Dome: American Orthodox Converts, Retreads & Reverts, Defeating Sin: Overcoming Our Passions and Changing Forever*, and *We Came, We Saw, We Converted.*

Fr. Joseph serves as priest at St. Joseph Antiochian Orthodox Church, Houston, Texas. He and his wife Elizabeth have three children: Mary Catherine, Basil, and Helen; a black cat named Lily; and a black standard poodle named Wotan (Hart).

Steve Robinson lives with his wife Peggy in Mesa, Arizona. They have a "Brady Bunch" of six children and three grandchildren. Steve has been a self-employed construction worker for over thirty years. He has assisted in establishing several mission churches and monasteries in Arizona and California. In his spare time he writes, podcasts, and draws for fun.

Other Recommended Reading

We Came, We Saw, We Converted
The Lighter Side of Orthodoxy in America
by Fr. Joseph Huneycutt
Based on his popular blog and Ancient Faith Radio podcast, *Orthodixie,* Fr. Joseph Huneycutt presents a humorous look at the pluses, minuses, joys, pitfalls, and struggles of perpetual conversion within an Orthodox Christian worldview. You'll be introduced to the lighter side of fasting, theosis, living a holy life in a secular world, and the struggle to understand those on the other side of the cradle/convert divide.

    For those days when acquiring the mind of Christ seems impossibly serious and, well, just plain impossible, a quick dip into *We Came, We Saw, We Converted* will restore your sense of humor and help you get up and try again.

• Paperback, 224 pages (ISBN: 978-0-9822770-8-9)
AFP Order No. 007729—$16.95*

Bread & Water, Wine & Oil
An Orthodox Christian Experience of God
by Fr. Meletios Webber
Worry, despair, insecurity, fear of death . . . these are our daily companions. It is precisely where we hurt most that the experience of the Orthodox Church has much to offer. The remedy is not any simple admonitions to fight the good fight, cheer up, or think positively. Rather, the Orthodox method is to change the way we look at the human person (starting with ourselves). Orthodoxy shows us how to "be transformed by the renewing of our mind"—a process that is aided by participation in the traditional ascetic practices and Mysteries of the Church. In this unique and accessible book, Archimandrite Meletios Webber first explores the role of mystery in the Christian life, then walks the reader through the seven major Mysteries (or sacraments) of the Orthodox Church, showing the way to a richer, fuller life in Christ.

• Paperback, 200 pages (ISBN: 978-1-888212-91-4)
AFP Order No. 006324—$17.95*

Help! I'm Bored in Church
Entering Fully into Worship in the Divine Liturgy
by David Smith

Do you ever find yourself feeling bored in church? Don't despair—you're not alone, and there is hope! Fr. David Smith offers four compelling reasons for going to church regardless of how we feel. He then explores

- six reasons people sometimes feel bored in church,
- five ways to think about your priest,
- four ways you can participate more fully in services,
- three kinds of waiting,
- two kinds of prayer, and the
- one thing truly needful in our relationship with God.

This book will help you see church as the best place you could possibly be—and the place you most want to be.
- Paperback, 136 pages (ISBN: 978-1-936270-64-4)

AFP Order No. 008425—$11.95*

Steps of Transformation
An Orthodox Christian Priest Explores the Twelve Steps
by Fr. Meletios Webber

Addictions and struggles with the passions are rampant in our culture. Fr. Meletios Webber, an Orthodox priest with a doctorate in counseling, helps us to understand addiction and explores ways to overcome it. He clearly and skillfully explains the Twelve Steps of the Fellowship of Alcoholics Anonymous. In correlating the Twelve Steps with basic Orthodox theology, Fr. Mel identifies the implications of the Twelve Steps for Orthodox, and for all Christians.

Using examples from the life of the Orthodox Church, he shows how the Steps can be a valuable resource for our spiritual journey.
- Paperback, 206 pages (ISBN: 978-1-888212-63-1)

AFP Order No. 006066—$14.95*

*Prices do not include applicable sales tax or shipping and handling. Prices were current on June 1, 2014, and are subject to change. To request a catalog, to obtain complete ordering information, or to place a credit card order, please call us at (800) 967-7377 or (219) 728-2216 or go to our website: store.ancientfaith.com.

Podcasts of Interest

Our Life in Christ
Join program hosts Steven Robinson and Bill Gould for an hour of insightful discussion about Orthodox Christian faith and practice. *Our Life in Christ* brings you the orthodox Christian faith as recorded in Scripture, taught and practiced by the early Fathers of the Church, and preserved within the spiritual life of the Orthodox Christian Churches around the world.

We record the program in Steve's basement lair and distribute it as a podcast, broadcast it on Ancient Faith Radio, and archive it on Our Life in Christ's website (http://ourlifeinchrist. com/).
• ancientfaith.com/podcasts/ourlife

Steve the Builder
A layman's view of living the Orthodox Christian Faith
Steve Robinson is heard regularly on *Our Life in Christ* with his co-host Bill Gould. But in this shorter podcast, Steve reflects on the practical side of being an Orthodox Christian working in a secular environment.
• ancientfaith.com/podcasts/stevethebuilder

Orthodixie
Homespun Wit and Wisdom from the Orthodox South
Fr. Joseph Huneycutt shares both his Southern wit and fatherly wisdom with each episode of this podcast.
• ancientfaith.com/podcasts/orthodixie

Lenten Retreat with Fr. Joseph Huneycutt
The 2010 Lenten Retreat at St. Vladimir's Seminary was held on March 20 and the speaker was Fr. Joseph Huneycutt. His three lectures were entitled *Paschal Fire from Spiritual Ashes* and include some of the material that was later incorporated into this present book.
• ancientfaith.com/specials/episodes/2010_lenten_retreat_-_ fr._joseph_huneycutt

Ancient Faith Publishing hopes you have enjoyed and benefited from this book. The proceeds from the sales of our books only partially cover the costs of operating our nonprofit ministry—which includes both the work of **Ancient Faith Publishing** (formerly known as Conciliar Press) and the work of **Ancient Faith Radio.** Your financial support makes it possible to continue this ministry both in print and online. Donations are tax-deductible and can be made at www.ancientfaith.com.

To request a catalog of other publications,
please call us at (800) 967-7377 or (219) 728-2216
*or log onto our website: **store.ancientfaith.com***

Bringing you Orthodox Christian music,
readings, prayers, teaching, and podcasts
24 hours a day since 2004 at
www.ancientfaith.com